UnityBuilder Devotions for Small Groups

Loveland, Colorado

UnityBuilder Devotions for Small Groups
Copyright © 2001 Group Publishing, Inc.

All rights reserved. No part of this book may be reproduced in any manner whatsoever without prior written permission from the publisher, except where noted in the text and in the case of brief quotations embodied in critical articles and reviews. For information write Permissions, Group Publishing, Inc., Dept. PD, P.O. Box 481, Loveland, CO 80539.

Visit our Web site: **www.grouppublishing.com**

Credits
Contributing Authors: Tim Baker, Karen Dockrey, Debbie Gowensmith, Michelle R. Hicks, Jan Kershner, Julie Meiklejohn, Todd Outcalt, Siv M. Ricketts, Christina Schofield
Editor: Amy Simpson
Creative Development Editor: Jim Kochenburger
Chief Creative Officer: Joani Schultz
Copy Editor: Pam Klein
Cover Art Director: Jeff A. Storm
Cover Designer: Ray Tollison
Cover Photography: Randy Pfizenmaier
Art Director: Jean Bruns
Designer: Ray Tollison
Computer Graphic Artist: Shelly Dillon
Illustrator: Matt Wood
Production Manager: Peggy Naylor

Unless otherwise noted, Scripture taken from the HOLY BIBLE, NEW INTERNATIONAL VERSION®. Copyright © 1973, 1978, 1984 by International Bible Society. Used by permission of Zondervan Publishing House. All rights reserved.

Library of Congress Cataloging-in-Publication Data

UnityBuilder devotions for small groups.
    p. cm.
  Includes index.
  ISBN 0-7644-2199-9 (alk. paper)
  1. Church group work with teenagers. 2. Christian teenagers--Prayer-books and devotions--English. I. Title: UnityBuilder devotions for small groups. II. Group Publishing.

BV4447 .U57 2000
268'.433--dc21
00-059304

10 9 8 7 6 5 4 3 2 1   10 09 08 07 06 05 04 03 02 01
Printed in the United States of America.

Contents

Introduction 5
Acts of Love 7
   Topic: *Love*
Bound in Unity 10
   Topic: *Friendship*
Boxed In 13
   Topic: *Problem Solving*
Bridges of Friendship 16
   Topic: *Friendship*
Building Bonanza 19
   Topic: *Friendship*
Candy Craze 21
   Topic: *Unselfishness*
Circle of Friends 24
   Topic: *Respect*
Common Bond Clues 27
   Topic: *Love*
Connected Acrobatics 30
   Topic: *Cooperation*
Crossword Conundrum 33
   Topic: *Problem Solving*
Eternal Encouragement 39
   Topic: *Encouragement*
Everybody Up 42
   Topic: *Unselfishness*
Foot-to-Foot Pass 44
   Topic: *Encouragement*
Fort Fun 46
   Topic: *Cooperation*
Geometric Designs 49
   Topic: *Cooperation*
Great Unknown 52
   Topic: *Problem Solving*
Group Hug 55
   Topic: *Love*
Hold On 58
   Topic: *Encouragement*
Jumping Jack Flash 61
   Topic: *Cooperation*

Contents

Lean on Me 63
  Topic: *Cooperation*
Loving Touch 66
  Topic: *Love*
Puzzling Problems 68
  Topic: *Problem Solving*
Reconciling Ties 71
  Topic: *Friendship*
Removing Obstacles 74
  Topic: *Servanthood*
R-E-S-P-E-C-T 77
  Topic: *Respect*
Safety Nests 81
  Topic: *Problem Solving*
Servanthood Splash 85
  Topic: *Servanthood*
Signed, Sealed, Delivered 87
  Topic: *Respect*
Stronger Than Thread 90
  Topic: *Friendship*
Survival 93
  Topic: *Servanthood*
Taste Test 97
  Topic: *Respect*
Tinfoil Teamwork 100
  Topic: *Unselfishness*
Tiny Power 103
  Topic: *Encouragement*
To the Top 106
  Topic: *Encouragement*
Tread on Me 109
  Topic: *Servanthood*
Unscrambled Scriptures 112
  Topic: *Respect*
Water Works 114
  Topic: *Unselfishness*
What's Mine Is Yours 116
  Topic: *Unselfishness*
When Talk Turns Tacky 118
  Topic: *Love*
Works of Art 122
  Topic: *Cooperation*
Indexes 124

Introduction

"Therefore, as God's chosen people, holy and dearly loved, clothe yourselves with compassion, kindness, humility, gentleness and patience. Bear with each other and forgive whatever grievances you may have against one another. Forgive as the Lord forgave you. And over all these virtues put on love, which binds them all together in perfect unity" **(Colossians 3:12-14).**

If your small group of teenagers is like most small groups of teenagers (and adults too), it could use some help in the unity department. Getting people to show up for youth meetings is one thing; getting them to live like the body of Christ is quite another. So where does unity come from? And how can you foster this precious quality among the young people you work with?

According to Paul's letter to the Colossians, an atmosphere of unity results when we strive to embody the virtues of compassion, kindness, humility, gentleness, patience, and most of all love as we work, play, and interact with one another. But this kind of atmosphere must be created deliberately and purposefully—unfortunately it doesn't just happen.

Your teenagers crave unity and belonging, but they don't always know how or where to find it. And in our mobile, technological society, interpersonal and social skills have fallen into disuse. People nowadays seem to find it very difficult to relate to one another and to understand what it means to belong—to be an important part of a group. That's where *UnityBuilder Devotions for Small Groups* comes in. The devotions in this book will benefit the teenagers in your group in three ways. First, the devotions bring young people closer to the God who created us and who wishes to live in unity with us. Second, the devotions help the members of your group grow closer to one another and begin to develop a sense of unity within the group. And third, the devotions help teenagers learn new ways of relating with others in their lives.

Each of the forty devotions in this book begins with a challenge activity. The activity may be a physically challenging problem that group members must work together to solve, or it may offer a mental challenge that requires students to "put their heads together."

The second part of each devotion is an opportunity for reflection and debriefing of the challenge activity. Then comes the "heart" of the devotion—students are given a Scripture to look up, read, think about, and apply to the activity they just experienced. Your group members will understand the rich wisdom of God's Word in new ways as they experience the concepts by challenging themselves and each other.

Any challenge activity, by its very nature, entails a certain degree of risk. Taking risks in a safe environment provides many opportunities for both personal and group growth.

Following are some ideas to help create a safe, yet challenging and fun, environment as your group experiences these devotions:

• Always practice "challenge by choice." Emphasize to students that they need to participate in activities only as much as they are comfortable. Ask students to respect and support one another in their decisions about how much or how little to get involved.

• On the flip side, encourage students to stretch their comfort zones and try activities that may be somewhat scary for them. It is only by stepping out in faith that we learn God will catch us.

• In activities that may involve some physical risk, ask other adults to act as spotters. The adult spotters will help teenagers feel safer and will eliminate students' fear of getting hurt during a challenge activity.

• All the activities in this book include ideas "For a Greater Challenge." Use these ideas with teenagers who want to take the challenges further.

• Get involved! Your students will learn so much more from the examples you provide than from the things you say. Enjoy and learn from the challenges of these devotions along with your youth.

• Most of all, have fun!

God's blessings to you and your youth group!

Acts of Love

Topic: Love
Scripture: Leviticus 19:18
Supplies: Bibles, gum or candy, wet wipes, paper, pens

[start] • • • • • •

Ask group members to find partners, then have students form two straight lines facing their partners. Say: **Do something kind for *yourself*, such as getting a piece of gum or candy, wiping your face and hands with a wet wipe, or stretching your muscles.**

When everyone has finished, ask:
- **How did you decide what to do for yourself?**
- **How did it feel to do something kind for yourself?**

Say: **Now do something kind for your *partner*, such as sharing some encouraging words, giving him or her a shoulder rub, wiping his or her face and hands, or giving your partner a piece of gum or candy.**

7

For a Greater Challenge

Take this activity to the next level by planning a meal with your students. Have students form pairs, and challenge them to focus their energy on meeting their partners' needs, by doing things such as refilling drinks or bringing additional servings of food.

Ask:

- **How did you decide what to do for your partner?**
- **How was this different from doing something kind for yourself?**
- **How can doing nice things for each other change our group?**

Have students open their Bibles to Leviticus 19:18. Ask a volunteer to read the verse aloud while the others follow along.

Ask:

- **How was doing something kind for yourself like loving yourself?**
- **How was doing something kind for your partner like loving your neighbor as yourself? How was it different?**
- **Who are your neighbors?**

Give students each a piece of paper and a pen, and ask them to fold their papers in half to make two columns. In one column, ask students to list ways that they demonstrate love for themselves. In the other column, ask them to list parallel ways that they could demonstrate love for their neighbors. For example, if one way they love themselves is by making sure they eat healthy foods, they could show love to others by making donations to a food bank.

Give students time to brainstorm eight to ten things for each list, then ask volunteers to share a few of their ideas.

Ask:

- **Is it easy or difficult for you to demonstrate love for yourself? Explain.**
- **Is it easy or difficult for you to demonstrate love for others? Explain.**
- **What would it take for you to be a more loving person, both toward yourself and toward others?**
- **What keeps us from showing love to ourselves or others?**
- **What can you do to overcome the things that prevent you from showing love for others?**
- **Do you have to feel love to demonstrate love? Explain.**

• **According to Leviticus 19:18, what stands in the way of loving others?**

Ask teenagers to silently consider whether they're holding grudges against others and, if so, how they can let go of the grudges in order to love other people. Allow for a brief time of silence.

Instruct students each to use a pen to draw a small heart on the back of one of their hands. Tell teenagers that they can use the hearts to remind themselves to demonstrate love for others.

[end] . . . . . .

Scripture

"Do not seek revenge or bear a grudge against one of your people, but love your neighbor as yourself. I am the Lord" (Leviticus 19:18).

Bound in Unity

Topic: Friendship

Scripture: Colossians 3:12-14

Supplies: Bibles, plate of cookies or another treat, several rolls of two-ply toilet paper, pens or pencils

[start] • • • • •

Before this exercise, put cookies or another favorite treat on a plate and set the plate at one end of the room. Then have group members gather together at the other end of the room.

Explain that the group is going to experience what it's like to be bound by the ties of friendship. Have students stand in a circle so they're all facing inward. Place several rolls of toilet paper in the center of the circle. Then tell teenagers to stand close together and loop their arms around the people next to them—almost like a group hug.

Explain that the group, from this position, will first need to bind itself in a cocoon of toilet paper. Tell group members you expect them to cover as much of themselves as possible without leaving large gaps between layers of toilet paper. Further explain that after the group has wrapped itself up, students will then need to walk together to the plate of cookies. Tell teenagers that during the walk, they must not rip the toilet paper. When the group has reached the plate of cookies, students must then unwrap the toilet paper without ripping it.

Encourage group members first to plan how they'll wrap themselves in the toilet paper since their arm movements will be somewhat restricted, and remind students that they should not rip the toilet paper. As students wrap themselves, encourage them to work together.

If someone drops the toilet paper and it lands out of reach, you can pick it up and hand it back to the student. If the toilet paper rips as the group is wrapping itself, students don't need to start over; instead, they can tuck in the ripped edge and continue wrapping with another piece.

If teenagers are having a hard time, here's a hint that might help them: A good way for the group to wrap itself in toilet paper without ripping it is for students to crouch to the same height, pass the toilet

paper behind themselves from person to person, then gradually stand up together as they wrap the toilet paper higher and higher.

When the group has wrapped itself up, have teenagers discuss how they'll move to the plate of cookies without ripping the toilet paper. A good way to do this is for students to plan their route and then elect a leader to count out small—very small—footsteps. If any group member feels unsteady, he or she can receive support from the people standing on either side.

When teenagers have decided on a strategy, encourage them to go slowly and carefully. If a little bit of toilet paper rips on the way, that's OK. However, if a lot of rips occur, have the group stop and mend their cocoon by tucking in the ripped areas before proceeding.

When the group reaches the plate of cookies, have teenagers stop and discuss how they'll unwrap themselves. A good way to do this is to reverse their strategy for wrapping themselves up. Tell the group to unwrap the toilet paper neatly. When teenagers have unwrapped themselves, congratulate them. Allow them to sit down and enjoy the treats. As they eat, ask:

• **What was it like being so close together as you tried to accomplish this task?**

• **What was required for you to successfully complete the activity?**

For a Greater Challenge

For groups in which members know each other fairly well, you can have the students form a circle facing outward. Since this formation doesn't allow groups face-to-face communication, both the planning and the walking stages are much more difficult.

- **What would have hindered you?**
- **How were the skills required to complete this task similar to those required for friendship?**

Ask a volunteer to read aloud Colossians 3:12-14 from a Bible. Then ask:

- **Which of the attributes in this passage is most important for helping friendships grow?**
- **How can you clothe yourselves with these attributes as you clothed yourselves with the toilet paper?**
- **How can these attributes bind us together even better than toilet paper bound us together?**
- **How can we encourage the growth of our friendships with one another?**

Distribute pens or pencils, and have each person tear off a square of toilet paper. Ask students to think about their behavior toward each group member and consider what they can do to encourage friendship and unity in the group. Have group members each write on the toilet paper one attribute from Colossians 3:12-14 that they most need to develop in their friendships. Encourage students to take home their ideas or place them inside their Bibles.

Close by allowing anyone who wants to pray aloud to do so, thanking God for the friendships in the group and asking for help in encouraging those friendships to grow.

Boxed in

Topic: Problem solving

Scripture: Ephesians 4:14-16

Supplies: Bibles, string, scissors, tape, about ten boxes of various sizes, two pieces of paper, markers, watch or clock

[start] • • • • •

Before students arrive, arrange your room:
• Clear out furniture and other obstacles as much as possible.
• Tape three pieces of string across the room, approximately parallel to each other, from one wall to the other. The piece of string in the middle should be waist-high and the other two pieces of string should be shoulder-high. The room will now be divided into four sections.
• Place the boxes at one end of the room in the first section. In the second section, securely tape two sheets of paper to the floor, evenly spaced apart.

The illustration below gives a general idea of the way the room should be set up. You may need to modify this activity depending on the size of your room and the number of students who will participate.

For a Greater Challenge

Do this activity in the dark, using flashlight beams to highlight the strings.

When all the students have arrived, tell them to stand by the boxes in the first section of the room. Say: **You work for a famous art dealer. He's loaning out some artwork, and he's asked you to load it onto a flatbed truck for shipment. The only problem is, he forgot to give you the code to the security system. You've got your artwork ready to load, but one of you has tripped the system. Now any movement will alert the police, causing a huge delay. You can't call your boss because he's out of the country. And if you don't get the artwork onto the truck in the next five minutes, you will all lose your jobs.**

The artwork is in these boxes in the first area. The second area has only two boards that haven't rotted away. They're the two sheets of paper, so you can only step on those. The third area is where you have to load the artwork. That area has a pressure-sensitive floor and motion detectors. The floor will only hold two people at a time without setting off the alarm. And you must move very slowly in that area. The last area is the truck itself.

You'll notice the sensor beams that are represented by the strings. The beam that's waist-high will trigger the alarm if anything touches the beam or crosses below it. The beams that are shoulder-high will trigger the alarm if anything touches them or crosses above them. You've got five minutes to load the artwork and yourselves onto the truck before it drives off. Go!

Give students exactly five minutes to move their boxes. When they've finished, congratulate students on their efforts. If students aren't able to complete this activity, you might want to give them another chance after suggesting ways they might do the exercise more effectively.

When students have finished the activity, tell them to gather in the third section of the room, the "loading dock."

Ask:

• **How would you grade our group's teamwork—A, B, C, D, or F? Why?**
• **How important is teamwork in our group?**
• **What does it take to develop teamwork?**

• **What group problems have we faced in the past?**
• **How have we handled these problems?**

Read Ephesians 4:14-16 and have students follow along.

Ask:

• **According to these verses, what things are important in solving problems?**
• **How can we become better at solving problems together?**
• **What role does unity play in problem solving?**
• **How can we become more mature, loving, and unified in our group?**

Have students gather around one of the boxes that you used in this activity. Give students markers and let them write ideas on the box for how they might work together as a group more effectively. For example, students might write "Get along better" or "Forgive each other." When group members have finished, let them each talk about what they wrote. When everyone has shared, have students spend time praying for one another and for the group. Encourage students to pray that group members will continue to work together to be effective problem solvers.

Scripture

"From him the whole body, joined and held together by every supporting ligament, grows and builds itself up in love, as each part does its work" (Ephesians 4:16).

Bridges of Friendship

Topic: Friendship

Scripture: Ephesians 2:19-22

Supplies: Bibles, swimming "noodle" toys cut into 2-inch sections (one "noodle" for every two students)

[start] ......

Toss the sections of the swimming "noodle" toys on the floor. Ask everyone to find a partner. Instruct partners to face each another, and ask students in each pair to place one hand palm-to-palm with one of their partner's hands. Explain that partners are to work together to build a bridge using the noodle sections. They will place noodle sections, one section at a time, between their palms.

For a Greater Challenge

If pairs of students are able to keep their noodle bridges together at longer lengths, ask them to bend down and touch their noses to the ground while keeping their bridges intact. Then have them stand up again, still keeping the noodle bridges connected.

Give students five to ten minutes to build their bridges, and encourage them to try to make the bridges as long as possible. Allow pairs to start over if their bridges fall during the challenge activity.

After students have finished the activity, have everyone sit down. Ask:

• **What was it like to build the noodle bridge with your partner?**
• **How did you need each other to get the job done?**
• **How is building a noodle bridge like building a friendship?**
• **What might the sections of the noodle represent in a friendship?**

Give each person a Bible. Have the group work together to find and read Ephesians 2:19-22. Ask:

• **What do these verses say about people who follow Jesus?**
• **What do these verses say about unity and friendship?**
• **How can we grow in our friendships with one another as a group?**
• **How can we become more unified as a group?**

Say: **These noodle pieces can represent experiences between friends. As friendships grow and change, there are a lot of little pieces that are involved; and the pieces of a friendship can hold friends together or push them apart.**

Ask:

• **What are some positive things these noodle pieces might represent that bring friends together?**
• **What are some negative things these noodle pieces might represent that separate friends?**
• **How do the positive experiences in a friendship make it stronger?**
• **How can the *negative* experiences in a friendship make it stronger?**
• **What does it take to develop a deeper friendship?**
• **Why do you think God gives us friends?**

Instruct teenagers to stand in circle. Have them hold up their hands with their palms out, touching the palms of the people on either side of them in the circle. Have teenagers go around the circle one at a time, and have them each place a noodle piece between their palm and the palm of the person next to them. As people do this activity, have them each name one way God is building friendships in the group. Continue to go around the circle, having group members take turns adding more noodle pieces. (You may need to help students add pieces.) With each piece added, teenagers should continue to name ways their friendships are strengthened and growing because of God's Spirit.

If a section of the group's noodle bridge breaks and pieces fall, have people name ways friendships in the group can be broken; then encourage group members to name ways to mend those broken bridges of friendship.

When everyone is connected by bridges, close in prayer. Pray that God will build and strengthen friendships among the students in the circle.

Scripture

"Consequently, you are no longer foreigners and aliens, but fellow citizens with God's people and members of God's household, built on the foundation of the apostles and prophets, with Christ Jesus himself as the chief cornerstone" (Ephesians 2:19-20).

Building Bonanza

Topic: Friendship
Scripture: Proverbs 18:24
Supplies: Bibles, old playing cards, rulers, pens or pencils, scrap paper, watch or clock, newspaper, glue sticks

[start] • • • • •

Have group members form pairs. If you have an uneven number of participants, join in forming a pair yourself. Give each pair a deck of old playing cards, a ruler, a pen or pencil, and scrap paper. (Old cards are often available in second-hand shops. You won't need a full deck for each pair, but each deck should have plenty of cards to work with.) Make sure the group has a flat surface on which to work. Then explain the challenge.

Say: **Your challenge is to construct a house out of the cards I've given you. Each pair is now a subcontractor, and each pair will be responsible for building a particular room of the house. The group will have to agree on the general layout for the house, and everyone will have to decide which pair will build which room. I'll give you a few minutes right now to discuss your plans. Then you'll have five minutes to build your house.** Give players about five minutes to discuss how to build the house.

Say: **Now it's time to start building! You'll have five minutes to construct your house. We'll see how far you get in that amount of time.**

Let students begin building the house. After five minutes, stop the building and survey the construction site. Have players assess the results.

Ask:
- **What was it like trying to build a house of cards?**
- **How was building this house of cards like trying to hold a friendship together?**
  - **Why was this challenge activity so difficult?**
  - **Why are friendships sometimes difficult to maintain?**
  - **What would have made this activity easier?**

For a Greater Challenge

To make this activity more challenging, have pairs try to build their card structures outside, weather permitting. Even the slightest breeze will add another degree of difficulty!

Say: **Let's try this activity again, but with a little help this time.**

Cover the construction site with newspaper. Give each pair a glue stick. Explain that pairs will have five more minutes to construct the rooms of the house, but this time they can use the glue sticks. Let the second phase of construction begin. Remind players to work together to build the entire house. After another five minutes, call time and let players admire their card house.

Ask:

- **Which house looked better, the first one or this one?**
- **How was construction the second time different from the first time?**
- **Just as the glue held the cards together, what is the glue that holds friendships together?**

Give each pair a Bible. Have partners work together to look up Proverbs 18:24.

Ask:

- **What does this verse say about true friendship?**
- **What's the difference between a companion and a friend?**
- **When is a time a friend has stuck by you? How did that make you feel?**
- **How can you be a better friend to someone this week?**
- **How can we stick together more as friends in this group?**

Have everyone hold hands around the card house. Close with a prayer asking God to help cement the bonds between the people in your group and to help them become the kind of friends who will stick together.

Candy Craze

Topic: Unselfishness
Scripture: 1 Kings 21:1-20
Supplies: Bibles, M&M's candies, bowl, paper towels, watch

start] • • • • •

Before you begin, you may want to ask students to wash their hands. Place a bowl of M&M's in the center of the room and give each person a paper towel.

Say: **You may each take a handful of candy, but don't eat it. Place it on your paper towel in plain sight.** When everyone has taken some candy, say: **You will have fifteen seconds to silently examine one another's candy. Then you'll have one minute to work together to be sure that each group member has candy of only one color. However, you may not touch your own candy.** If you have more than six students, it's OK for more than one person to have candy of the same color.

Give students fifteen seconds to look at the candy, then signal students to begin the activity. After one minute, ask:

• **Do you have more or less candy now than when you started?**
• **Are you satisfied with the amount of candy you have now? Why or why not?**
• **How was this activity like real life? How was it different?**

Ask students to open their Bibles to 1 Kings 21:1-20. Take turns reading a few verses each until you've read the whole passage. Then discuss these questions for each of the three characters:

• **How willing might Naboth, Ahab, or Jezebel have been to give away M&M's? Explain.**
• **At the beginning of the story, was this character content with what he or she had? Why or why not?**
• **What happened in the story to increase or decrease Ahab's and Jezebel's contentment?**

Continue by discussing these questions:

• **What does it mean to be unselfish?**
• **Which of the Bible characters behaved selfishly? unselfishly? Explain.**

For a Greater Challenge

Ask students to sit in a circle with their candy in front of them.

Say: **Your goal is to be sure each group member has candy of only one color, but you can't speak while you're playing.** [Student's name] **will begin by putting all but one color of his or her candy on a paper towel and passing it to the person on the left. For example,** [student's name] **might keep only the red candy. The next person will then take all the candy of a different color, say blue, from the paper towel. Before passing it on, he or she can add only candy of *one* other color, for example, yellow. You'll need to watch who has taken and given up what colors to know which colors you should take. Keep going until each person has only one color of candy.**

Time how long it takes students to accomplish their goal. Allow them to try again to see how quickly they can do it.

- Why do you think people so easily choose to behave selfishly?
- In your experience, what are the results of selfish actions? unselfish actions?
- What's the relationship between selfishness and contentment?
- With which character in the story do you identify the most? the least? Explain.
- How could unselfishness affect your friendships? our group unity?

Say: **One way we can become less selfish is by praying for others. We give to them our prayers, and God blesses us by changing our attitudes. Based on the color of candy you have, you'll be asked to pray for a group of people.**

Assign groups to students as follows:
- Red prays for family members.
- Orange prays for friends.
- Yellow prays for people at school.
- Green prays for people at church.
- Blue prays for people in leadership positions.
- Brown prays for people in other countries.

Starting with red, ask students each to pray silently for their own family members, then allow the student with the red candies to pray aloud a general prayer for that category of people. Continue with the next color. Again have students each pray silently, then have the student with that color M&M's conclude with a spoken prayer. Continue until the group has prayed for each category. If you have fewer people than categories, cover the remaining categories in a general closing prayer at the end. For example, if you don't have students assigned to people in leadership or people in other countries, ask teens to silently pray for both categories, then lead students in a spoken prayer. If you have more than one person with a particular color of M&M's, have both students pray aloud for that category.

[end] . . . . . .

Scripture

"Ahab said to Elijah, 'So you have found me, my enemy!'
'I have found you,' he answered, 'because you have sold yourself to do evil in the eyes of the Lord' "
(1 Kings 21:20).

Circle of Friends

11/4/01

Topic: Respect
Scripture: Mark 10:35-44
Supplies: Bibles, masking tape, watch

[start] • • • • •

Before this challenge activity, use masking tape to mark a circle on the floor in the center of the room. Make the circle about twelve inches in diameter. Then gather all the group members around the tape circle.

Say: **Think about how you could fit the feet of everyone in the group inside this tape circle without touching the circle. Discuss the question as a group and give me one idea.**

Have everyone sit in an area away from the circle to discuss the problem and come up with an answer. After the group gives you its answer, have everyone stand around the circle again.

Say: **Let's see if you're right. When I give the signal, I want everyone to fit his or her feet inside the tape circle on the floor. Whoever doesn't get his or her feet inside the circle loses. Are you ready? Go!**

Stand back as players scramble to fit their feet inside the circle. To encourage competition—and even a little pushing and shoving—remind teenagers that players who don't get their feet inside the circle will lose. Be careful not to let the game get out of hand, though. Call time after about one minute.

Players may not be able to accomplish this challenge—yet! If they do figure it out, challenge them to try to find a way to accomplish it without sitting. At the end of the devotion, players will get another chance to figure out the challenge.

Have group members sit in a circle around the tape outline. Ask:

• **What was it like trying to get all of your feet inside the circle?**

• **How did you feel about your fellow group members as you tried to complete this challenge?**

• **How was pushing to get inside the circle like how we sometimes treat others in selfish and disrespectful ways?**

For a Greater Challenge

See if group members can figure out the solution to the challenge without giving them any hints.

• **How does this activity remind you of competitive situations in real life?**

Say: **Turn to someone sitting near you and describe a situation you've faced recently that involved the kind of behavior you just saw in this activity.**

Give group members several minutes to share their experiences, then ask volunteers to share their responses with the rest of the group. After volunteers have described their recent experiences, give each person a Bible. Have group members help each other find and read Mark 10:35-44. You may want to have one group member read the passage aloud as other members follow along in their Bibles.

After the group has finished reading, ask:

• **How was trying to get into the circle like how James and John wanted to be first with Jesus?**

• **What does Jesus say in this passage about wanting to be first?**

• **When are times you see people pushing to be first or most important in a situation? How do you react?**

• **How would the results of this challenge have been different if you had asked others to put their feet into the circle first?**

- How does putting others before ourselves show respect for others?
- How could we show more respect for each other within this group?
- How would your life be different if the people around you—at school, at home, and here in this group—showed more respect for one another? How would *the world* be different?

Say: **Let's do this challenge again, but this time we'll see if we can be more respectful toward one another.** Have players stand around the tape circle again, then say: **Now that you know to put others before yourself, try again to get all your feet inside the circle.**

Give players another chance at the challenge activity. Feel free to offer hints as needed. (The solution is for students to sit down and pile their feet on top of each other's feet.) When players are seated with their feet inside the circle, close with a group hug, asking God to help everyone show more respect to each other.

[end] . . . . .

Scripture

"Whoever wants to become great among you must be your servant, and whoever wants to be first must be slave of all" (Mark 10:43b-44).

Common Bond Clues

10/28/01

Topic: Love
Scripture: 1 John 4:7-21
Supplies: Bibles, pens or pencils, one photocopy of the "Common Bond Clues" handout (p. 29) for each person

[start] • • • • •

Give each person a copy of the "Common Bond Clues" handout (p. 29) and a pen or pencil. Explain that students should try to figure out the common bond between the four things listed in each set. Allow five to ten minutes for students to solve the questions as a group and write the answers on their handouts.

When the students have finished, offer the answers in the key below.

Answer Key

1. Types of trees
2. Types of cards
3. Types of picks
4. All have blades
5. All have feathers
6. All have a king
7. Types of paper
8. All have a beard
9. All can be opened
10. All have a ring
11. Types of shoes

Ask someone to read 1 John 4:7-21 aloud. Say: **One thing we all have in common is that we are recipients of God's love and mercy. Christ died even for people who are unkind or sinful, and he wants us all to learn to love him in return.**
Ask:
• **According to this passage, how should we respond to God's love for us?**
• **Why do you think God loves us so perfectly?**

For a Greater Challenge

Ask each student to develop a "common bond" puzzle with four items. Collect the puzzles, read them aloud, and encourage the group to try to solve them.

Have students read 1 John 4:10 silently, then ask:

- **What do you think is the most amazing characteristic of God's love?**

Ask students to take a few minutes to write parables that characterize God's love for people. Invite them to work with partners and write their stories on the backs of their handouts. After several minutes, allow volunteers to share their stories aloud.

Ask:

- **What difference has God's love made in your life?**
- **How does loving God change people?**

Say: **Think of someone who loves you unconditionally.**

Ask:

- **How do you feel around this person?**

Say: **The confidence to be yourself and to improve yourself often comes when you feel accepted as you are. Each of us, by really loving others, is capable of making a profound difference in people's lives.**

Ask:

- **What things can you do to help bring out the best in the people in this group?**

Say: **The passage we read earlier tells us it's impossible to love God if we don't love the people around us.**

Ask:

- What's the connection between our love for God and our love for one another?
- How can we demonstrate our love for God by loving other people?

Close by saying: **By caring about people simply because they are important to God, we are helping those people become who God wants them to be, and we're showing our love for God. Unconditional love gives people the freedom to try new things and to grow.**

Common Bond Clues

Find the common bond in each of the word sets listed below.

1. palm, Christmas, apple, pear

2. phone, greeting, credit, post

3. ice, tooth, guitar, draft

4. windshield wiper, grass, knife, ice skate

5. chickens, ducks, boas (garment, not the snake), pillows

6. monarchy, deck of cards, bowling pins, mattresses

7. toilet, news, recycled, notebook

8. Santa Claus, Abraham Lincoln, Rip van Winkle, Uncle Sam

9. can, envelope, door, window

10. groom, boxing, collar, telephone

11. ballet, tap, dress, tennis

Permission to photocopy this handout from *UnityBuilder Devotions for Small Groups* granted for local church use. Copyright © Group Publishing, Inc., P.O. Box 481, Loveland, CO 80539.

Connected Aerobatics

Topic: Cooperation
Scripture: Philippians 2:1-4
Supplies: Bibles, string, scissors

[start] • • • • •

Have group members stand in a line, shoulder to shoulder. Give each person two pieces of string. Have students each tie their right ankle to the left ankle of the person on the right. Then ask students each to tie their right wrist to the left wrist of the person on the right (teenagers may need help tying the strings). You'll end up with one long line of people who are tied together at their ankles and their wrists.

Say: **Today we're going to study how well we work together as a team. To demonstrate this, I'm going to give you objectives from three different categories. I'd like you to work together as a group and do as many of these as you can. The tasks will start out easy, but they'll get more difficult.**

Have students do the activities in the following list. Assign both activities from each difficulty level, and give students time to complete the activities.

Low Difficulty
- Make a heart
- Make a star

Medium Difficulty
- Make a group pyramid
- Do somersaults

High Difficulty
- Carry half the group to the other end of the room and back
- Do the Hokey Pokey

When students have finished, ask:
- **How did you feel trying to do these activities while tied together?**

• **How important was cooperation to succeed in these activities?**

• **How important is cooperation between members of our group? Explain.**

• **When have you experienced a lot of cooperation in our group? Discuss.**

Ask students to disconnect from the group in pairs so that pairs of people are still tied together. Ask pairs to try a few of the activities they tried in the larger group. When they have finished, let students untie themselves.

Read Philippians 2:1-4 aloud as students follow along in their Bibles. Then ask:

• **How are unity and cooperation connected?**

• **Why were unity and cooperation important to Paul?**

• **Why do you think unity and cooperation are important to God?**

• **Why is cooperation important in our group?**

• **What are some barriers to cooperation?**

Say: **We need to cooperate as a group on whatever projects we're attempting. We need to join together at completing our tasks and work together as a team. We'll accomplish more, and we'll please God.**

For a Greater Challenge

Take your group on a field trip while everyone is tied together. Have teenagers travel in a van or another vehicle that allows them to remain tied together and still use seat belts. Then go to a fast food restaurant, a mall—almost anywhere will work—and complete an assigned task together. You might have teenagers shop for a specific item or have a meal together.

Have students stand in a circle and hold hands. Ask students to pray aloud, asking God to help group members cooperate with one another.

[end] . . . . .

Scripture

"If you have any encouragement from being united with Christ, if any comfort from his love, if any fellowship with the Spirit, if any tenderness and compassion, then make my joy complete by being like-minded, having the same love, being one in spirit and purpose" (Philippians 2:1-2).

Crossword Conundrum

Topic: Problem solving

Scripture: James 1:5; 1 Corinthians 1:20-25

Supplies: Bibles, dictionaries, pens or pencils, photocopy of the "Crossword Conundrum Puzzle" handout (p. 36) and the "Crossword Conundrum Clues" handout (p. 37)

[start] • • • • •

Before this activity, make a copy of the "Crossword Conundrum Puzzle" handout on page 36 and the "Crossword Conundrum Clues" handout on page 37. Enlarge the puzzle "frame" to the biggest size possible. The goal is to have one large copy of the crossword that everyone in the group can work on together. If that's not feasible, make two copies of both the puzzle and the clues, and let members form two smaller groups to work on the puzzle. If players must form two groups, encourage the groups to work together during the challenge activity.

Gather everyone around a table with good lighting, and set out pens or pencils to share. At first you'll hand out just the crossword puzzle "frame" without the word clues that tell how to solve the puzzle.

Say: **I have a problem-solving challenge activity that will test your vocabulary skills—plus your knowledge of the Bible!** Give the group the copy of the crossword puzzle *without* the clues.

Say: **This crossword puzzle has some very good advice from the Bible about how to solve problems—see if you can find the Bible verse in this crossword puzzle!**

It probably won't take long for group members to realize that solving the crossword is impossible without further information. As soon as someone *asks* for the word clues to help solve the crossword, give the group the copy of the clues. Don't give the group the clues until someone actually asks for them with a question. If no one phrases the request as a question, ask leading questions to help group members form a question. For example, you might say, "I hear your frustration, but how can I help? What exactly are you asking?"

For a Greater Challenge

To make this activity more challenging, don't provide dictionaries. You could also see if players can identify the Scripture reference of the verse without looking it up in a Bible.

After someone asks for the word clues, give players the copy of the "Crossword Conundrum Clues" handout. Also supply a couple of dictionaries and several Bibles for reference. (The specific wording for the verse used here is from the Holy Bible, New International Version.) Remind students that the crossword puzzle contains a Bible verse that gives good advice about problem solving. Then let players fill in the crossword puzzle to reveal the verse. Give players as much time as necessary to solve the puzzle. For your convenience, the crossword puzzle solution is printed on page 38.

After group members solve the puzzle, tell them to find James 1:5, and have everyone read the verse aloud. Then ask:

- **What keeps us from asking God for wisdom?**
- **According to James 1:5, what happens when we do ask God for wisdom?**

Then read 1 Corinthians 1:20-25.

Ask:

- **How is God's wisdom different from our wisdom?**
- **How was this difference illustrated in your two attempts at solving the crossword puzzle?**
- **How was this activity like the problems we sometimes face in real life?**
- **How could we better handle the problems we face in life?**

Say: **Sometimes we may feel as though we don't have a clue how to solve a particular problem. But the Bible tells us in James 1:5 that all we have to do is ask, and God will give us wisdom. And there's no reason to approach life relying only on our own wisdom when God's amazing wisdom is available to us.**

Ask:

- **How does God give us wisdom?**
- **When has God helped you solve a problem?**
- **How can we, as a group, help each other turn to God when we're faced with problems?**

Say: **Many people say there's a method to solving crossword puzzles—once you've solved one or two puzzles, you become** familiar with the words and clues the puzzles use. Then the crosswords are easier to solve. It's the same way with God. Once we become used to asking God for help, we learn to recognize his wisdom—without a lot of searching. We learn to rely on the Holy Spirit and recognize his voice in our lives.

Have everyone stand in a circle and close with a prayer, asking God to help each person in the group learn to ask God for wisdom when faced with a problem.

end] . . . . .

Scripture

"Where is the wise man? Where is the scholar? Where is the philosopher of this age? Has not God made foolish the wisdom of the world?" (1 Corinthians 1:20).

Crossword Conundrum Puzzle

Hidden verse:

Crossword Conundrum [Clues]

Across

1. Lacking
3. Blame
6. Derived from
7. Contained by
8. Duty
10. Synthetic material
11. End of the arm
12. Thing
13. Lord
15. Adult male
17. To request
18. Handed over
19. Sick
21. Freely and in abundance
24. Which person?
25. On condition that
27. Also
28. Sea snake

Down

1. Knowledge
2. Toward
3. Discovering
4. No matter which
5. Two thousand pounds
9. Does not have
11. Masculine pronoun (objective)
13. Bestows
14. Bear's home
16. Everything
19. Hotel
20. To exist
21. Suitable
22. Fruit skin
23. Who are ____?
24. Last testament
26. Masculine pronoun (nominative)

Crossword Conundrum [Solution]

	1W	i	t	h	o	u	2t			3f	4a	u	l	5t
	i					6o	f		7i	n				o
8s	h	o	9u	l	d				10n	y	l	o	n	
d			a		11h	a	n	d						
o			c		12i	t		i			13G	o	14d	
15m	16a	n	k		m			n			i		e	
	l		17a	s	k			18g	i	v	e	n		
19i	l	l				20b					e			
n			21g	e	n	e	22r	o	u	s	l	y	23	
n		24w	h	o			25i	f					o	
		i					n						u	
26h		l			27a	n	d							
28e	e	l												

The verse hidden in the crossword...

The verse hidden in the crossword is James 1:5 (wording from the Holy Bible, New International Version).

Permission to photocopy this handout from *UnityBuilder Devotions for Small Groups* granted for local church use. Copyright © Group Publishing, Inc., P.O. Box 481, Loveland, CO 80539.

Eternal Encouragement

Topic: Encouragement

Scripture: 2 Thessalonians 2:16-17

Supplies: Bibles; various recreational supplies and other equipment, such as soccer balls, footballs, basketballs, tennis balls, Hula-Hoops, in-line skates, tennis shoes, jackets, suitcases, flags, and toys; a stopwatch; strips of paper; pens or pencils

[start] • • • • •

Place the recreational supplies and other equipment at one end of the room. Ask teenagers to line up single file at the other end of the room. Explain that the group is going to play a game to see how many of the items they can accumulate and carry.

The first person will run to the other end of the room and pick up one item. He or she will run back and hand the item to the next person in line. The second person will run to the other end of the room carrying the item and pick up an additional item. He or she will run back and hand both items to the next person in line. Continue with each person in line picking up another item and then handing all the equipment to the next person in line. If a person drops any of the items, he or she must pick up the items and continue the game.

As students begin the game, start the stopwatch. Let the group know you're keeping track of time to see how fast they can accomplish the task. When the last item is carried back to the starting line, the game is over and the clock is stopped.

Ask:
- **Was this game difficult or easy? What made it that way?**
- **What motivated you to continue playing and not give up?**
- **What were the positive things you did as a team?**
- **How does encouragement make a team stronger?**

Give each person a Bible. Have the group work together to find and read 2 Thessalonians 2:16-17.

Ask:
- **What do these verses say about encouragement?**
- **What encourages your heart?**

For a Greater Challenge

When the last person has carried all the items to the starting point, have each person in the group try to carry all the items across the room and back.

- How does encouragement from others give you strength?
- What is eternal encouragement?

Say: **The Christians who first read this letter received an inner strength and peace that encouraged them because Jesus had given them eternal life. Although they may have faced difficult times just like we do, they knew that one day these problems would end and they would be with Jesus. Their words and actions reflected the peace, strength, and encouragement they felt.**

Ask:

- **What are some of the problems that weigh us down or make our lives difficult?**
- **What are some ways we can help one another carry the load and deal with these problems?**
- **How can we encourage and strengthen one another?**
- **How does encouragement from others affect the way you feel and act?**
- **How has someone encouraged you during the past month?**

Say: **Life is sometimes hard. When we're feeling low, we need encouragement from others. When we're feeling up, we need to share the hope inside us with others and encourage others.**

Have students sit in a circle. Instruct each person to choose one of the items used in the opening game and to think about one of the struggles he or she is facing right now. For example, a person on the football team might pick up a football to represent the problems he is having making good grades. His poor grades may hurt his standing on the team and may affect whether or not he can play the rest of the season. Another person might pick up in-line skates and then share that her family is having problems—the student's parents aren't "in line" with each other, and their problems affect the whole family. After a student has shared, he or she should return the item to the pile.

Whatever teenagers share, encourage them to be open and honest about their struggles. As students each share their problems, ask the other group members to give words of encouragement. Another student might want to share that he or she is having the same struggle and tell something that has encouraged him or her.

Be aware of the fact that some students may share some very serious struggles, such as suicidal feelings or abuse at home. Be prepared to deal with these types of issues if they arise.

After everyone has shared at least one problem and has received encouragement, ask:

• **How do you feel about your problems and struggles now, after you have shared them and received encouragement from others?**

• **Why is it sometimes difficult to share problems and receive encouragement?**

• **What are some ways God has encouraged you?**

• **How do you feel about God and others when they listen to you and encourage you?**

Say: **God wants us to give our struggles and problems to him. He wants to encourage us. God wants to remind us that no matter what we face, he's there for us. No matter what we go through in this life, our Christian friends can encourage us and help us through the tough times. We can read the Bible and see for ourselves how much God loves us and wants to encourage us every day. As God encourages us, we'll be able to encourage one another even more.**

Give teenagers the strips of paper and pens or pencils. Ask them each to write the names of everyone in the group. Then have students write beside each name a special word of encouragement for that person.

Say: **God believes in us, and he wants us to believe in other people. God wants us to believe in their abilities and gifts. He wants us to believe that he has a special plan for each person's life. When we believe in others the way God does, it's easy to find positive things to say to them. Even though we may know these positive things about someone, we need to encourage that person and show through our words and actions that we believe in that person.**

Close in prayer, asking group members to first pray silently about how they can encourage others in the group through their words and actions. Then invite students to share their words of encouragement (from their pieces of paper) with each other. Challenge group members to encourage one another this week with phone calls or by sending cards.

Topic: Unselfishness
Scripture: 1 John 3:16-17
Supplies: Bibles

[start] •••••

Tell students that this activity will require them to demonstrate unselfishness as they work together to complete a simple task. Ask them what they think acting in an unselfish manner means. Have teenagers describe times they've acted unselfishly in order to accomplish a goal.

Then ask each student to find another student who is roughly the same size as he or she is. Have partners sit on the floor facing each other with their knees bent and the bottoms of their shoes touching. Tell teenagers that when you say "go," they'll each need to grab their partner's hands tightly and try to stand up. Give pairs time to do the activity, then ask:

- **How did you solve this problem?**
- **How did this task require you to be unselfish?**
- **What would have happened in this activity if one partner had acted selfishly?**
- **Why is it important to act unselfishly when you're working as a member of a group?**

Give everyone a Bible, and have the group read 1 John 3:16-17. Ask:

- **Christ gave us the supreme example of acting unselfishly. What do these verses tell you about acting unselfishly?**
- **According to this passage, why is it important to act unselfishly and to look out for one another?**

Say: **"Laying down our lives for our brothers"** doesn't necessarily mean that we need to die for our friends or family members. It may mean that we need to give up our time, our plans, or other things that are important to us in order to show support to people we love.

For a Greater Challenge

Have students sit on the floor in a large circle with their legs extended. Explain that you'd like group members to try to stand up at the same time. Give the group a few minutes to master this task, and then have everyone sit down.

Ask:
- **What are some examples of things you might need to give up...**
   if someone in this group is feeling left out?
   when a person in the group needs to talk about a problem?
   if someone in this group is having money problems?
   when a group member is feeling overwhelmed with too much to do?
   if a person in the group gets sick?

Close by having partners stand back to back and lean on each other as they share ways they will strive to act more unselfishly within the group.

end] . . . . .

Scripture

"This is how we know what love is: Jesus Christ laid down his life for us. And we ought to lay down our lives for our brothers" (1 John 3:16).

Foot-to-Foot Pass

Topic: Encouragement

Scripture: 1 Thessalonians 5:9-11

Supplies: Bibles; several balls of various sizes such as a table tennis ball, a soccer ball, a beach ball, and a football; stopwatch or watch with a second hand

[start] ● ● ● ● ●

Have teenagers stand in a circle about one foot apart from each other. Next place a soccer ball on the floor between the feet of one player. Let this person choose which direction he or she will start the ball around the circle. Explain that the ball must be passed around the circle, behind and between each person's feet, as illustrated below.

For a Greater Challenge

Every now and then, blow a whistle to signify that teenagers must change directions with the ball. If you want to keep the group on its toes, sound the whistle several times during the game.

The object is for players to work together to move the ball around the circle as quickly as possible. When the ball returns to the starting point, the round is over. Then players will begin the next round, doing the same thing with another ball. Time each round, and see if the group can beat its previous record. Repeat the game several times using balls of different sizes, shapes, and weights. Playing with a football may be especially interesting!

After the game is over, ask:

• **What was encouraging about this game?**

• **How would this game be different if you were the only one trying?**

• **How have others encouraged you? What was that like?**

• **What are some things people could do or say that would most encourage you in your daily life?**

Read 1 Thessalonians 5:9-11 as students follow along. Ask:

• **What point are these verses making?**

• **How should we treat each other as fellow Christians? Why?**

• **After reading this passage, what changes could we make in our group?**

Have group members form pairs. Ask students in each pair to think of one encouraging statement they'd like to share with another pair in the room. Then have partners go to that pair and share their encouragement.

When teenagers have finished, ask:

• **How did it feel to share encouragement?**

• **How did it feel to receive encouragement?**

• **Why do you think God wants us to encourage one another?**

• **How can we be more encouraging to others in this group?**

Have students sit with their partners and spend time praying, asking God to help them encourage others.

Fort Fun

Topic: Cooperation
Scripture: Exodus 35:4–36:7
Supplies: Bibles; blindfolds; a watch; furniture such as chairs, tables, or couches; two or three large sheets

[start] • • • • •

Explain to group members that their goal is to build a fort in five minutes. Then tell teenagers these rules:
• They may use anything they can find in the room including the furniture and the sheets you've provided (or you may want to allow them to use anything in the entire building).
• They must try to design the fort so that all group members can sit inside the fort and no one will be visible from outside it.

Explain to the group that, in addition to the preceding rules, each person must choose from the following list a way he or she will participate in building the fort:
• Some group members must be blindfolded, use only one arm and hand, and may not speak during the activity.
• Some group members can use only one leg and foot, and they can't speak during the activity.
• Some group members can *only* speak and use their eyes.

Tell students they must include representatives from each of the categories. In other words, all the students cannot choose to be in the same category.

Instruct students to begin by planning together how they'll build the fort. Remind students to include in their discussion the special considerations they'll have to make based on how each group member will participate. Let teenagers know it's important that every group member has at least one job to do. During the planning stage, teenagers may not touch any building materials, but they may speak and use their eyes.

After teenagers have taken about five minutes to plan, distribute blindfolds. Have students blindfold the group members who won't be able to use their eyes. Remind the group of the rules, including the

For a Greater Challenge

Have group members build the fort in the dark. Allow them to plan the fort with the lights on, but then turn off the lights before they begin building. Give only one person a flashlight.

---

rules about how each person may participate. Then give the group five minutes to build the fort.

As students work, watch and encourage them. If the group becomes frustrated or too disorganized to continue, have everyone stop what they're doing, take a deep breath, and briefly assess the plan they made and how it's working. It's OK if the group decides to alter the plan during the building process.

When the group has built the fort and is satisfied with the work, have everyone sit inside it. Allow the blindfolded students to remove their blindfolds. Congratulate the group members on their work. Then ask:

- **What would it have been like for one person to complete the task alone?**
- **What was it like for everyone to work together?**
- **How was each person important in completing this task?**
- **What kinds of things prevent us from cooperating?**

If the group faced difficulties in building the fort, be sure to ask debriefing questions about those experiences, too. For example, ask:

- **How did the problems you had to deal with affect your feelings of cooperation?**
- **What are some frustrating things about working with a group?**
- **How do the benefits of group cooperation compare with the difficulties of working together?**

After the discussion, give each student a Bible. Ask group members to read aloud Exodus 35:4–36:7, and let each person have an opportunity to read.

Afterward, ask:

- **What does the Israelites' experience communicate about cooperation?**
- **What differences have you noticed between times when people work individually and when people work cooperatively?**
- **When have you experienced that kind of cooperation in your life?**
- **How can we encourage that kind of cooperation in our group?**

Tell the group that it's time to take down the fort and that the restrictions under which they built the fort no longer apply. However, with each item students remove from the fort, they must name a skill or characteristic that they or another student can cooperatively use within the group.

After the group has disassembled the fort and returned all the building materials to their original locations, have everyone stand in a circle. Show students how to shake hands by reaching with your right hand to the person on your left while reaching with your left hand to the person on your right. If all group members cross their arms this way, students around the circle will be able to shake hands with the people standing next to them.

Have students continue holding hands, and close with a prayer. Ask God to help the group cooperate more, and thank God for the enjoyment and power we get from cooperation.

[end] . . . . .

Scripture

"All the Israelite men and women who were willing brought to the Lord freewill offerings for all the work the Lord through Moses had commanded them to do" (Exodus 35:29).

Geometric Designs

Topic: Cooperation

Scripture: Ephesians 4:2-6

Supplies: Bibles, one blindfold per person, one long rope (it should be long enough so that there's about two feet per person, with a minimum of ten feet)

[start] • • • • •

Before teenagers arrive, place the rope out of sight. When you're ready to begin, ask students to stand in a circle and give a blindfold to each person. Instruct everyone to put on the blindfolds. When group members are blindfolded, place the rope on the floor in the middle of the circle.

Say: **Pick up the rope from the floor, and I want all of you to hold on to the rope with both hands. We're going to make geometric shapes using the rope. Let's begin by making a triangle.**

49

For a Greater Challenge

Ask group members to create more complicated geometric shapes. For example, have teenagers create a pentagon or an octagon. You might also ask participants to create other shapes, such as a heart or a star.

Let the group work together to form a triangle with the rope. They may talk to one another, but they must remain blindfolded. When the group members agree that they've made a triangle, allow them to remove their blindfolds and see their design. Then ask the students to put their blindfolds back on.

Say: **Now instead of making a triangle, we're going to make a circle. Again, every person must hold the rope with both hands as you make the circle.**

Allow the group time to form a circle with the rope. When the group members think that they've made a circle, allow students to take off their blindfolds and see the design. Then have the group members put on the blindfolds one more time.

Say: **We've made a triangle and a circle. Now let's make a square. Every person needs to hold the rope with both hands.**

Allow the group time to make a square. When teenagers agree that they've formed a square with the rope, allow group members to take off their blindfolds. As the students hold the rope in a square, ask:

- **How were we able to work as a group to make the shapes?**
- **How could we have done better as a group?**
- **How did cooperation among the group change with each shape?**

Say: **Cooperation is a big part of keeping unity within a group. Even though we may sometimes disagree, we can all still cooperate to accomplish the task. Sometimes cooperation will come easily and at other times it will take more effort.**

Ask:

- **How do we keep a spirit of cooperation when we don't necessarily feel like cooperating with others?**

Give each person a Bible. Have the group find Ephesians 4:2-6, and ask a volunteer to read the verses aloud.

Ask:

- **What are suggestions given in these verses to help people learn to cooperate with one another?**

- **How difficult or easy is it to keep unity among people? Why?**
- **Although we're all different, what are the main things that motivate Christians to cooperate?**

Pick up the rope and ask everyone to hold on to the rope with both hands. Say: **Although we're all individuals, separate and different, there is one thing that ties us together as Christians. Our hope, our faith, our belief in Jesus is the rope that connects us to one another. Jesus is the reason we cooperate with one another. When our hearts and minds are in tune with God's desires, we more willingly work together to accomplish his plans. We don't worry so much about our personal opinions and desires, but instead we cooperate and compromise at times to keep the unity of the Spirit.**

Ask:
- **How can our group members become more cooperative with one another?**

Without the blindfolds, have the group form the geometric shapes again. First ask students to form a triangle, then a circle, and finally a square.

Ask:
- **How was it different to form the shapes without the blindfolds?**

Say: **When our eyes are open to the needs of others in our group, we tend to be more patient and gentle and to bear with one another in love, as it says in Ephesians 4:2. When our eyes are open to God's Spirit, represented by the rope, we see how we're all connected in spite of our differences.**

Ask:
- **What are some ways we can keep our eyes open and know the needs of others in our group?**
- **What are some ways we can keep our eyes open to God's Spirit?**

Close by asking everyone to grab the rope with both hands and form a circle. Pray that the group members will stay connected with one another because of their relationships with Jesus. Pray that they'll continue to learn cooperation as they work and learn together as a group. Pray that Jesus will remain the cord that binds the group together.

Great Unknown

Topic: Problem solving
Scripture: Jeremiah 33:3
Supplies: Bibles, toothpicks, large marshmallows, felt-tip pens

[start] • • • • •

Before this activity, create a model using toothpicks and marshmallows. Use approximately ten toothpicks, and connect the toothpicks with marshmallows to form a geometric model. Hide the model until group members arrive. When everyone has arrived, explain that one student will be allowed to see the model and then that person will explain the model to the others in the group.

Ask one student to look at the model quickly (for about ten seconds), then hide the model. Provide the group with toothpicks and marshmallows, and instruct the student to lead the group in building an exact replica of the model. The group members can ask questions, but the student can answer only "yes" or "no" to the questions. And the student cannot touch the replica that the other group members are building.

As the teenagers build the model, check their frustration level. If necessary, allow an additional person to see the original model. When the group members feel they have successfully built the replica, show them the original.

For a Greater Challenge

Instead of using only toothpicks and marshmallows, build a model using additional items. For example, use marshmallows and clay to hold together toothpicks and pencils. Participants will try to copy the model exactly, so have the additional items available. Then see if students can put the toothpicks, pencils, and other items in the correct places.

Ask:
- **How well did you do on the model? Why?**
- **What would have made the building process easier?**
- **How well do you think you worked together as a group?**
- **What were your strengths as a group? your weaknesses?**

Read Jeremiah 33:3 aloud and have students follow along in their Bibles.

Ask:
- **What does God promise us in this verse?**
- **What are some ways we can call to God?**
- **What are some ways God answers us?**

Say: **In this activity, you had a problem to solve—you were trying to build a model just like the one I had built.**

Ask:
- **What are some problems we can call on God to help us with?**

Say: **When we call to God, he'll give us an answer. Sometimes the answer is yes and sometimes it's no. Sometimes God doesn't give us all the answers at one time. Sometimes we have to continue seeking God's direction and calling for help. Often God gives us the answers we need when we read the Bible— God's Word. At other times God uses Christian friends, teachers, and even our parents to reveal his answers.**

Ask:
- **What are some problems God has helped you solve in the past?**
- **Who or what method did God use to lead you to the answer?**

Say: **God wants to help us as we go through our lives. God wants to give us the answers we need to solve the problems we face each day. God wants to show us his plans and purposes for how we should live. Sometimes we will have God's answer or direction, and we'll be like the person who saw the original** model firsthand. When this happens, we need to share the things God has taught us with the rest of the group.

Ask:

• **What are some other ways we can work together to solve problems within our group?**

• **How can we work together to seek out God's answers to our individual problems?**

Give two students about one minute to build another model using toothpicks and marshmallows. Then have the other group members try to build an exact replica of the model without seeing it. But this time, allow the two students who built the model to share more information and to answer questions with more than just "yes" or "no." When the group members think they have completed the model, compare the model with the original.

Ask:

• **How was solving the problem different this time?**

• **How does communication and sharing information help the problem-solving process?**

• **How can we share the information and answers God gives us as individuals and make a difference in our youth group?**

Give each person a toothpick, a marshmallow, and a felt-tip pen. Ask students to draw pictures on their marshmallows to symbolize their commitment to unity and problem solving within the group. For example, someone might draw two hands clasped together to symbolize working and sticking together to solve problems. Another person might draw a cross to show that the group is committed to solving problems in a Christlike way.

Explain that you're going to close with a group prayer. Each person will connect his or her toothpick and marshmallow to another person's marshmallow to form a new group model. This new model will be one that each person in the group can see and take part in building. As each person connects his or her piece, that person will say a one-sentence prayer for the group. Encourage students to pray for group unity. Pray that as a group and as individuals, people will call to God for help in solving problems. Pray that they'll trust and depend on one another as they struggle with various problems in the future.

Group Hug

Topic: Love
Scripture: 1 John 3:18
Supplies: Bibles, one blindfold for each person

start] • • • • •

This activity works best outside in an open field with few obstructions, such as in a sports field or a yard with few trees and bushes. Your students will be blindfolded, so be sure you'll be able to keep your group members away from streets or parking lots. If part of the playing field borders a potentially dangerous area, station yourself near that area during the game to steer teenagers away.

If you'd rather conduct the activity inside, use a large, open room such as a gym. However, you can also do the activity in a classroom or a room in a house as long as the furniture can be moved to the edges of the room. While you don't need a completely empty space, keep in mind that students will be walking while blindfolded. You'll definitely want to move aside those priceless vases and porcelain lamps.

Explain to group members that they're going to do a big group hug to show how much they love one another. After the groans have subsided, explain that you've got some different rules for this particular group hug.

Take students to the area in which they'll play the game, and have everyone gather together in the center of the area. Distribute blindfolds to all the students. Before participants put on the blindfolds, point out the boundaries of the playing area. Explain that if anyone crosses the boundaries, you'll either steer that person back into the area or call out "freeze!" If you call out "freeze," everyone is to stand still until you say "unfreeze."

Have students put on their blindfolds. Then invoke a rule of total silence. Emphasize that people may not talk, stomp their feet, hum a tune, belch, or otherwise make noise during the game. Tell students you're going to lead each person, one by one, until he or she is standing alone. When everyone is positioned, you'll begin the game by calling out, "Show your love with a big group hug!"

For a Greater Challenge

During the game, play music and dim the lights (or do this activity at dusk). You want to provide enough light so you can prevent any accidents, but the reduced amount of light will further disorient the group members. By playing music, you'll mask the background noises of walking, making it more difficult for students to find one another.

Students should then begin walking around *slowly* in an effort to find the rest of the group. When a person finds someone else, those two people should link elbows. Then without saying a word, those people should together search for others. Whenever teenagers find other people, they should link elbows and continue searching together. The goal is for the entire group to become linked together.

Tell the students that when all group members are linked together, you'll call out "group hug!" and the participants must engage in a group hug—still without speaking.

When everyone understands the rules, remind students again about the rule of silence. Then take each student, one by one, to stand alone in the game area. It's a nice touch to spin each student around a few times to disorient him or her. You don't need to arrange all the students around the periphery; just be sure they're evenly spread out.

After you've placed everyone, call out "Show your love with a big group hug!" Then watch carefully as students wander around. If a student near you crosses a boundary, simply steer him or her back into the game area. If a student farther away crosses a boundary, yell "freeze!" Then go to the student and steer him or her back into the game area before yelling "unfreeze!"

As students wander, remind them to walk slowly and carefully so they won't bang into each other or any other obstacles. Also encourage teenagers to hold their arms out in front of them as they walk.

When all the students have linked elbows, call out "group hug!" After the group has joined together for a hug, have students sit down and take off their blindfolds. Tell teenagers they can talk again.

Ask:

• **What was it like to show your love to one another without speaking?**

• **How was completing this activity different from simply talking about your love to each other?**

• **Do you agree that actions speak louder than words? Explain.**

• **How is showing love different from just talking about it?**

Distribute Bibles, and have students look up 1 John 3:18. Ask a volunteer to read aloud the Scripture.

Then ask:

• **What does it mean to love with actions? to love in truth?**

• **What difference does it make to you when people show you they love you with actions and in truth?**

• **What kinds of things can we do to show that we love each other in truth?**

Have group members each think of one creative (and appropriate) way they can show love for one another in the group. For example, group members can pray for each other, talk to each other, smile at each other, and so on. Spend the last couple of minutes allowing students to show their love to each other in the ways they've thought of. Then have students gather in a circle, and close in prayer, thanking God for showing us love and for showing us how to love one another.

Hold On

Topic: Encouragement
Scripture: Hebrews 3:12-14
Supplies: Bibles

[start] • • • • •

Before you begin this activity, make sure the center of your room is cleared of obstacles. Have group members form a single-file line in the center of the room with students standing one behind the other. Have players stand with their legs about three feet apart.

Refer to the illustration below. Have the first player in line bend over and reach back between her legs with her right hand to grasp the left hand of the player behind her. Have the other players each reach behind them to grab the next person's hand. Explain that when you give the signal, the last player in line will lie on his back, putting his feet between the legs of the person in front of him. Then the next player will lie down, and so on, as the students walk backward, straddling their teammates lying on the floor. Eventually everyone will be lying down.

For a Greater Challenge

To make this activity more challenging, perform several rounds of the challenge activity and see if the group can do the activity faster each time.

When everyone is lying on the floor, the player who began the challenge as the first person in line will now be the person lying at the end of the line. Then that player at the end of the line will stand up, pulling up the next player after her, and walking forward as she straddles the players on the floor. Each player will follow along until all players have returned to their original positions. Tell players that the challenge is to perform the whole sequence while still holding hands.

When players understand the instructions, signal the start of the game. Encourage players to move slowly, since time is not a factor. If people let go of one another's hands, tell players to grab hold again and resume play. When group members successfully perform the challenge, have everyone sit in a circle on the floor.

Ask:
- **What was easy about this challenge? What was difficult?**
- **What was the trick to being successful in this challenge?**
- **Was it easier to lie down or pull each other up? Why?**
- **How was holding on to each other's hands like encouraging each other in life?**

Give each person a Bible. Have group members find and read Hebrews 3:12-14.

Then ask:
- **What does this passage say about encouragement?**
- **How was holding on during our challenge like encouraging each other during good times and bad?**
- **When is a time you needed encouragement from a friend? Did your friend come through for you? Explain.**
- **Do you find it easy to ask for encouragement? Why or why not?**
- **What would this challenge activity have been like if I hadn't explained the directions first?**
- **How is that similar to the way we sometimes don't let others know we need their help?**

Say: **Sometimes our friends may not even know we're facing a situation in which we need encouragement. And sometimes** those people who are closest to us don't let us know how we could help them.

Ask:

• **What could you do this week to be a more encouraging friend or family member?**

• **How could we be more encouraging in this group?**

Have group members stand in a circle, holding hands crisscrossed across their bodies. Go around the circle and ask each person to say a one-word description of a situation in which he or she needs encouragement right now. For example, group members might say "health," "school," or "relationships." Close with a prayer asking God to help group members pray for and encourage each other during the coming weeks.

[end] . . . . .

Scripture

"But encourage one another daily, as long as it is called Today, so that none of you may be hardened by sin's deceitfulness" (Hebrews 3:13).

Jumping Jack Flash

Topic: Cooperation
Scripture: 1 Peter 4:8-11
Supplies: Bibles, long jump rope or piece of rope

start] • • • • •

Before doing this activity, clear an open space in the center of the room. Explain to group members that they're going to be "flashing back" to childhood and playing a unique jump-rope game. Give teenagers a long jump rope or a long piece of rope. Ask two students to turn the rope, and have them turn the rope at a consistent speed. Encourage other group members to take turns practicing their jump-rope skills by jumping through the rope as the students turn it. Have each person jump through the rope several times before the activity begins.

After people feel comfortable jumping, say: **Your job is to get everyone in the group to jump through the turning jump rope once. Sounds simple enough, right? The catch is that every time the rope turns, there must be a person jumping. If the rope makes one complete turn without someone jumping, the group must start over. The students turning the rope must jump, too, so some of you need to be ready to take over turning the rope so those students can jump through.**

Once everyone understands the rules, begin the challenge. If the rope turns completely without a person jumping, have the group start over. Notice who in the group emerges as leader, that person's leadership style, the successful strategy that the group uses, and how group members treat one another throughout this activity. Be sure to provide encouragement when needed, but don't help group members solve the problem.

After the group has completed the activity, ask:

• **What was it like to get everyone through the rope in this activity?**

• **What was your strategy to make this happen?**

• **How did you feel about the leadership others provided during this activity?**

• **How did group members treat one another?**

For a Greater Challenge

Have group members jump in pairs or trios. You may even want to try having the whole group jump at once!

- How did you feel about the way you treated others?
- Why was it important to work together in this activity? **What happened** (or would have happened) **if you didn't work together?**

Give everyone a Bible, and have the group find and read 1 Peter 4:8-11.

Ask:

- What part of this passage appeals to you most? Why?
- What does this passage tell you about cooperation?
- What are some other components of cooperation that aren't mentioned in this passage?
- Did you feel that members of the group demonstrated these things in the activity we just completed? Give some examples.
- How can we use what we discovered about ourselves as a group during the activity and the information in this Bible passage to make our group work together better?

Have each group member hold on to the jump rope, and say: **Just as we're all connected to this rope, we're also all connected to one another. It's important to remember to work together so no one gets left out.**

Lean on Me

Topic: Cooperation
Scripture: Ecclesiastes 4:9-12
Supplies: Bibles

[start] • • • • •

Explain to students that they're going to do an exercise in which they'll need to cooperate with each other in order to be successful. Ask students to share what they think cooperation involves and why it's important to cooperate. Have students tell about times in their lives when they've had to cooperate with others in order to achieve a goal.

Then have students form a circle and hold hands. Have each student stand with his or her feet shoulder-width apart, and make sure students are standing far enough apart so that their arms are stretched out. Tell each student to make sure he or she feels balanced and comfortable.

For a Greater Challenge

Have group members try to switch positions without letting go of each other's hands. Students who are leaning backward will try to lean forward and those who are leaning forward will try to lean backward.

Ask students to count off by twos around the circle. (The first person will count "one," the next person will say "two," the third person will say "one," and so on.) When everyone has been assigned a number, tell students that in a moment you'll say "lean." When you say "lean," the Ones should slowly lean backward and the Twos should slowly lean forward. Tell students that they should lean without bending at the waist and should be careful not to pull or twist each other's arms. Make sure that everyone understands the activity and then say "lean."

Encourage teenagers to slowly lean forward or backward as far as they can. If group members cooperate with each other and trust each other, each student can exert a strong force on the students he or she is connected to. This can allow some remarkable leans forward and backward.

When students have done this, have Ones and Twos switch roles so that the Ones will lean forward and the Twos will lean backward. Again, encourage students to lean slowly without bending at the waist. When they have finished the activity, have students sit down and ask:

- **What was this activity like for you?**
- **Which did you find more challenging—leaning forward or leaning backward? Why?**
- **Why was it important to cooperate with each other during this activity?**
- **What would have happened if even one person didn't cooperate? Explain.**
- **What else did this activity require?**
- **This activity required both trust and cooperation. How do you think the two are related?**

Give everyone a Bible, and have the group work together to find and read Ecclesiastes 4:9-12.

Ask:

- **What does this passage tell you about cooperation?**
- **What part of this passage do you think most fits the activity we just completed? Why?**

- The last verse says, "A cord of three strands is not quickly broken." What do you think this means?
- This passage discusses the importance of friendship. How do you think trust and cooperation are important in friendships?
- How well do you think the members of our group work together with trust and cooperation?
- Are there certain areas we all could work on? If so, what are they?

Have each student find a partner and share one way he or she can help to improve the trust and cooperation within the group. When partners are finished sharing, have them link arms with each other. Then have pairs link arms with other pairs until the whole group is linked.

Say: **When we cooperate and work together, it links us more closely to each other in God's name. Let's pray together and ask God to help us continue to trust each other and cooperate with each other as we do his work in the world.**

Close by leading the group in this prayer: **Dear Lord, thank you for each and every member of this group. Please help us work together and trust one another more every day. We know that if we cooperate with one another, we can accomplish your work in the world. We pray in Jesus' name, amen.**

Loving Touch

Topic: Love
Scripture: John 15:12-17; 1 Corinthians 13:4-7
Supplies: Bibles, long rope or clothesline cord, stopwatch

[start] • • • • •

Begin by asking the teenagers to grab on to a long rope or clothesline cord with both hands. Explain that each person in the group must somehow touch every other person in the group at least once (not necessarily using their hands or at the same time), and everyone must keep both hands on the rope at all times. Tell players that you'll time them, and they need to complete the challenge as fast as possible. The students will be forced to work together to bend and circle around each other—while still holding on to the rope. Not everyone can be touching at the same time, but it is possible to accomplish the task by cooperating.

After the group has worked together to complete the activity, challenge students to try it again and to do it even faster.

Ask:
- **What made this challenge difficult?**
- **How are the difficulties you faced in completing this activity like challenges we sometimes face in showing love to others?**

For a Greater Challenge

You can make this activity more challenging by setting a time limit. Also the shorter the rope, the more difficult this activity becomes.

Following this preliminary discussion, have everyone form a circle. Distribute Bibles, and ask someone to read aloud John 15:12-17. Then ask:

• **How would you summarize what Jesus was teaching about love?**

• **How is the type of love Jesus is speaking of different from how people usually think of love?**

• **How, according to Jesus, might love challenge us or change us?**

• **Why do you think Jesus placed so much importance on loving one another?**

• **How do you see this type of love demonstrated in Jesus' life?**

Have one or two volunteers read aloud 1 Corinthians 13:4-7. Ask the students to talk among themselves and come up with a list of the qualities of love mentioned in this passage. Invite three or four of the teenagers to express these qualities in their own words.

Then ask:

• **Which of these qualities of love do we most readily see in our group? Which qualities are more difficult to find in our group?**

• **What makes them challenging to live out in our group?**

• **In our daily lives, how can we demonstrate the qualities of love mentioned in this passage?**

• **How can we demonstrate these qualities when our group gets together?**

• **How might the power of love be a changing force in our group?**

• **Can you think of people who might need to know of our love today? How can we show them our love?**

• **How might we be able to help by loving someone who is facing a difficult situation?**

Following this discussion, close by inviting the group to offer the words of 1 Corinthians 13:4-7 to each other by reading the Scripture passage aloud in unison.

Puzzling Problems

Topic: Problem solving
Scripture: James 1:5-8
Supplies: Bibles, index cards, pens or pencils

[start] • • • • •

The following puzzles require a dialogue between you and your students. Read each puzzle, then allow students to ask you questions in order to solve the puzzle. The only answers you may give are "yes," "no," or "not related." Encourage teenagers to work together to solve the puzzles.

Be aware that creative problem solving can be a frustrating experience. Your group may be tempted to give up and ask you for the solution to a puzzle. Don't give in too soon! Letting teenagers sit with their discomfort may prompt them to reach the level of creativity they need to think of the right questions to ask. Go on to the next puzzle if you need to. Sometimes simply applying the mind to a different task will open up the necessary space for new thoughts. Also this will challenge students to think about how easily they might give up on solving problems in their own lives.

Four puzzles are outlined below. Start with one puzzle and move on to the next one after students solve the first one.

The Carrot and the Scarf

Puzzle: A carrot and a scarf are lying on the lawn. Nobody put them on the lawn, but there is a perfectly logical reason why they should be there. What is it?

Solution: They were used by children who made a snowman. The snow melted and left behind the carrot and the scarf.

Push That Car

Puzzle: A man pushed his car. He stopped when he reached a hotel, at which point he knew he was bankrupt. Why?

Solution: He was playing Monopoly.

The Blind Beggar

Puzzle: A blind beggar had a brother who died. What relation

For a Greater Challenge

After working through the puzzles in this activity, ask students to form pairs and have students write their own puzzles and solutions. Then have pairs present their puzzles for the other teenagers to solve.

was the blind beggar to the brother who died? (Brother is not the answer.)

Solution: The blind beggar was the sister of her brother who died.

Fish in the Forest
Puzzle: A beach ball and the body of a fish were found deep in the forest. The nearest lake was eight miles away, and the ocean was one hundred miles away. How did the beach ball and fish get in the forest?

Solution: During a forest fire, a firefighting plane had scooped up some water from the lake to drop on the fire. The plane had accidentally picked up the fish and the beach ball and dropped them in the forest.

Continue working on the puzzles for about ten minutes, then ask:
• **Were these puzzles easy or difficult? Explain.**
• **Why was it important to ask questions in trying to solve the puzzles?**
• **Was it helpful to work together to solve these puzzles? Why or why not?**
• **When might you need creative problem solving in your life?**
• **How did you feel while trying to solve these puzzles? How is that like or unlike how you feel while solving problems in your life?**
• **Were you tempted to give up? Why or why not?**
• **When are you tempted to give up on the puzzles you face in real life?**

Instruct students to open their Bibles to James 1:5-8. Ask a volunteer to read the passage while the others follow along.

Ask:
• **How would you define wisdom? Why is wisdom important?**
• **How does this passage characterize God? Why is that important to problem solving?**

• Why do you think this passage puts so much emphasis on belief?

• How might God use other people to help you solve the puzzles you face in real life?

Distribute index cards and pens or pencils. Ask each student to write down one confusing situation or question in his or her life. Encourage teenagers to think about personal situations in which they really need God's wisdom, not philosophical questions. Let students know you'll be reading the cards aloud. When everyone has written a situation or question, collect the cards.

Shuffle the cards, then read them one at a time, being careful to keep the identity of the writers confidential. After you read a card, ask students to share any advice they have for the person who wrote the card.

After the cards have been read and discussed, have students form pairs.

Say: **We're going to spend some time in prayer now, asking God for wisdom and trusting that God will give it to us. Pray with your partner about specific problems for which you need wisdom.**

After several minutes of prayer, close by asking God to grant your group wisdom and that God would reveal to group members how they can support each other and help each other through confusing times.

Scripture

"If any of you lacks wisdom, he should ask God, who gives generously to all without finding fault, and it will be given to him" (James 1:5).

Reconciling Ties

Topic: Friendship
Scripture: Romans 5:6-11
Supplies: Bibles, four chairs, two pieces of string, paper, pens or pencils

[start] • • • • •

Clear a space in the middle of the room, then set out four chairs to form a square. Tie a piece of string about waist-high to two of the chairs. Tie the other piece of string to the other two chairs so that the room is divided into thirds by the strings. Ask two students to stand in the middle part of the room between the strings, then have the remaining students divide up equally in the other two parts of the room. (If you have an uneven number of students, you may want to join your students in doing this activity.)

For a Greater Challenge

Give students in the center section a minute to strategize before they begin helping others over the string. When the minute is up, have students begin, but ask teenagers to remain silent until everyone is in the center.

Tell the two students in the middle that it's their job to get everyone over the strings into the center section. Students on the sides can't help themselves, but once over the string, they assume the job of helping others into the center. As more people arrive in the middle section, they must work with others in the center section to help other students over—there should be no solo operators. Be sure teenagers understand that this is not a competition to see which group can get into the middle first.

Allow students as much time as it takes to accomplish the task. When everyone is in the center, ask:

• **What was it like to have to depend on someone else for help?**

• **What was it like to work together to help others?**

• **The two groups outside the strings were separated. What things separate people in life?**

• **What might bring people who are separated together?**

Have students form pairs and read Romans 5:6-11. Distribute paper and pens or pencils, and ask pairs to write six sentences—one sentence to summarize each verse. This will help students get a better understanding of the passage. Or you could assign each pair one or two verses to summarize.

When pairs have finished, ask students to share their sentences, going verse by verse through the passage.

Ask:

• **How would you define reconciliation?**

• **In our activity, how did those in the middle section reconcile those on the sides?**

• **How is that like or unlike what Jesus has done for us?**

• **How do you feel knowing that, through the work of Jesus, God has become your friend?**

• **What implications does this have for your friendships? for our group?**

Ask students to share with their partners a time they needed someone to help them reconcile a relationship. When teenagers have finished, ask them to share one way that they experience friendship with God.

Then ask students to sit in a circle. Untie the pieces of string from the chairs, and tie the pieces together to make one long string. Grab one of the ends and wrap the string once around one of your wrists as you say: **We can think of Jesus reconciling us to God like Jesus taking string and linking us to God. We can be reconcilers in our friendships with each other, working to establish new connections and to reestablish connections that have been broken. As you wrap the string around your wrist, share one way you can be a reconciler in our group. If you need to reconcile with someone here, you can take this opportunity to do so. Then pass the end of the string to another person.**

With the string still wrapped around your wrist, hand the excess string to the person next to you. Ask that person to wrap it once around one of his or her wrists while sharing. Then have that student pass the string to the next person until all the students' wrists are connected.

Close with a prayer, thanking Jesus for his reconciliation, and asking for the courage and strength to imitate him in reconciliation.

end] . . . . .

Scripture

"For if, when we were God's enemies, we were reconciled to him through the death of his Son, how much more, having been reconciled, shall we be saved through his life!" (Romans 5:10).

Removing Obstacles

Topic: Servanthood
Scripture: 2 Corinthians 6:3-10
Supplies: Bibles, pens or pencils, index cards

[start] • • • • •

When the students arrive, have them form two teams. Tell the teams they will use the classroom furniture to design an obstacle course for the other team to maneuver through. In addition to using furniture, students may use their own bodies to make part of the obstacle course. Allow a few minutes for students to plan and discuss how they will set up the course, then ask one team to create its course while the other team turns away or steps into another room. Then have the second team return to the room and find its way through the obstacle course created by the other team.

After everyone on the team has attempted the course, allow the second team to create its course for the first team. You may want to allow students multiple runs through the course until they complete it successfully.

When both teams have run an obstacle course, ask teenagers to work together to put the furniture back where it belongs.

Ask:

• **What was it like to put obstacles in front of the other team?**

• **How do people do this to each other in life?**

• **What are some obstacles you feel that others have put in front of you?** (If necessary, remind students to be discreet—this is not an opportunity for students to gossip.)

• **How was working together to put the furniture back in place different from the obstacle courses?**

• **In real life, which do you think you do most: put barriers in front of people or take them down? Explain.**

• **Which would you rather do? Why?**

Ask students to open their Bibles to 2 Corinthians 6:3-10 and take turns reading a verse at a time until they've read the whole passage.

74

For a Greater Challenge

If you have time, arrange to take your group to a challenge course, such as a ropes course or a climbing wall. Local camps, conference and retreat centers, or the YMCA might have adventure facilities, or these organizations might be able to refer you to a place that has such facilities. Local sports or camping stores might also be able to recommend places. Before you go, ensure that students fill out the appropriate medical release forms and insurance forms.

Say: **In this passage, Paul listed a number of situations that could have been obstacles to his ministry. For example, endurance (verse 4) isn't an obstacle, but perhaps someone created an obstacle to Paul's ministry that he had to endure. On the other hand, troubles (verse 4) could have been an obstacle if Paul had approached situations with a bad attitude.**

Have teenagers find partners, and assign each pair one or more verses from 2 Corinthians 6:4-10. Ask pairs to discuss these questions about each potential obstacle in the passages:

• **Could this have been an obstacle others put in front of Paul and his ministry? If so, how?**

• **Could this have been an obstacle Paul put in the way of others believing in his ministry? If so, how?**

Give pairs several minutes to discuss the questions, then starting with verse 4, ask students to share what they discussed.

Then ask:

• **What do you think it means to be a servant?**
• **What does servanthood have to do with removing obstacles?**
• **Why was Paul concerned with stumbling blocks?**
• **What does this passage tell you about servanthood?**
• **Why should you want to be a servant?**

Give each pair of students pens or pencils and several index cards.

Say: **Share with your partner a time you acted as a servant. What obstacles did you need to avoid in being a good servant? After you've both shared, brainstorm several ways you could be servants in our group. Write one act of service on each index card.**

As students finish, collect the cards in a pile. Ask teenagers to close their eyes. Say: **Silently consider servanthood.** (Pause.) **I'm going to ask some questions, and I'd like you to answer them silently, just to yourself.**

Ask:
- **Do you think you're a servant in this group? Why or why not?** (Pause.)
- **What obstacles are in your way in becoming a better servant?** (Pause.)
- **What would it take to remove those obstacles?** (Pause.)

Say: **In order for our group to grow in unity, we need to be willing to act as servants for one another. Like Paul, that means we'll experience hardships for each other and with each other. But if we are motivated to serve each other out of service for God, God will be faithful in supporting us through even the hardest situations.**

Set out the index cards you collected earlier. Say: **If you're willing to commit to servanthood in this group, open your eyes and take an index card. Then write one specific way you will follow through this week on that act of service.**

You might consider keeping the extra index cards. For the next several weeks, challenge students to take a new card each time your group meets and encourage students to follow through on the acts of service.

Scripture

"We put no stumbling block in anyone's path, so that our ministry will not be discredited. Rather, as servants of God we commend ourselves in every way" (2 Corinthians 6:3-4a).

R-E-S-P-E-C-T

Topic: Respect

Scripture: 2 Chronicles 19:7; Romans 2:11

Supplies: Bibles; boxes, chairs, tables, and other items to build an obstacle course; bandanas (one for each person); paper; pens or pencils; balloons; markers

[start] · · · · ·

Set up an obstacle course using boxes, chairs, tables, and other items. Explain that teenagers will work together to get through the obstacle course as a team as fast as they can. They must also line up in a certain order and must remain in that order throughout the entire obstacle course.

Ask students to line up according to their birthdays, from January through December. After everyone is lined up, give each person a bandana. Then assign each person a body part to tie the bandana around. For example, you might have one person tie a bandana around his or her arm and have another person be blindfolded. Explain that the body part where the bandana is tied is "immobilized" and that students cannot use those body parts as they go through the obstacle course.

For a Greater Challenge

You may want to tie more than one bandana on each person or on several people. For example, you might tie bandanas around both legs and both arms of one person. The team will then have to work together to carry this person through the obstacle course.

When you give the signal, have teenagers begin their race through the obstacle course. Remind them to work together as a team to get everyone through the course. Continue to provide encouragement as students work together and complete the course.

Ask:
- **How did you like the obstacle course?**
- **What was the most challenging part of the course for you?**
- **How did you have to work together to get everyone through the course?**
- **Did you feel like you were a valuable part of the group? Why or why not?**
- **Did you feel like the group members respected one another in spite of their weaknesses** (the bandanas)?

Say: **To respect someone is to value him or her. When you respect someone, you look to him or her as an important person, and you treat that person with consideration. When you work together as a group to accomplish a task, you show respect to one another. Although it might have been easier to go through the course one at a time, by working together everyone was successful.**

Ask students to find 2 Chronicles 19:7 in their Bibles. Have a volunteer read the verse aloud. Then ask students to find Romans 2:11 in their Bibles, and have a volunteer read the verse aloud.

Ask:
- **What do these verses say about respect?**
- **What do these verses tell us about God?**
- **What do you think God wants us to learn from these verses?**

Have teenagers form two groups. Give each group about five minutes to make up a short skit (one minute or less) with two endings. The first ending should reflect what happens when we fail to respect one another. The second ending should show how things are different when we respect one another. For example, a group might create a skit in which someone is voicing an opinion. In one ending, the rest of the group ridicules the person and refuses to listen to him or her. The person feels rejected and leaves the group. In the second ending, group members listen to the person's opinion and ask questions to make sure they understand. Then other group members take turns voicing their opinions and listening to one another. Everyone learns something, and everyone stays in the group.

After each group has had time to make up a skit, allow groups to present their skits.

Ask:

• **How did the characters in the skits fail to show respect to others?**

• **How did the situations turn out differently when the characters were respectful?**

• **What are some ways we can be more respectful of one another in our group?**

• **How can respecting one another strengthen our group?**

• **Who are other people in our lives we can show respect to?**

Give each person a sheet of paper, a pen or pencil, and a balloon. Ask teenagers to tear the paper into strips. Have students write on the strips of paper the names of people they need to show respect to. Have them include the name of everyone in the group who is at the meeting. Next to each person's name, encourage students to write one way they'll show respect to that person this week.

When teenagers have finished writing on their strips of paper, have each student fold his or her strips and stuff all of the papers inside his or her balloon. Then have the students blow up their balloons and tie them. Distribute markers and ask each person to draw a face and write his or her name on the balloon.

Say: **"Face-receiver" is a literal translation of a Greek word for respect.**

Ask:

• **What do you think "face-receiver" means?**

Say: **God wants us to accept and receive people, no matter what they look like. God wants us to respect others for who they are as his creations. God wants us to receive people, respect them, and accept them. When you look at your balloon face, remember that God wants you to receive the faces—the people—whose names are written on strips of paper inside your balloon. God wants you to respect these people, and that includes respecting everyone in this group.**

Close in prayer by having teenagers stand in a circle, holding their balloon faces with their names on them. Ask people to pass the balloons to the person on their right. Then instruct students each to pray a simple, one-sentence prayer for the person whose balloon they're holding.

Have students continue passing the balloons around the circle to the right and praying for the people whose names are on the balloons until everyone has prayed for each person in the group. Conclude by praying aloud, asking God to help group members respect one another as well as show respect to others outside the group.

[end] . . . . .

Scripture

"Now let the fear of the Lord be upon you. Judge carefully, for with the Lord our God there is no injustice or partiality or bribery" (2 Chronicles 19:7).

Safety Nests

Topic: Problem solving
Scripture: Romans 12:3-8
Supplies: Bibles, drinking straws, Easter grass or straw, duct tape, raw eggs

start] • • • •

Plan to do this activity outside, if possible. The group will be designing "nests"—complete with raw eggs—and will be dropping the nests from a height. Consider setting up a ladder, or plan to have students drop their nests out of a second- or third-story window. If a ladder or high window isn't available, have students stand outside and toss their nests onto a hard surface about fifteen feet away. Don't use a soft, grassy area, however, because the activity won't be nearly as challenging.

If you can't do this activity outside, set up a ladder, have students gather at the top of a staircase, or have students toss their nests from one point to another. Be sure to have group members drop the nests onto a hard surface—a cement floor or tile floor, for example—rather than onto a carpeted surface.

If you do this activity indoors, you'll also need to plan for the possibility that some eggs might break. For easy cleanup, tape trash bags or a tarp in the area where students will be dropping the nests.

Set out drinking straws, Easter grass, duct tape, and whole raw eggs with unbroken shells. Explain to group members that you have a problem you'd like them to solve. Tell students that countless young birds are lost every year when nests fall from trees, breaking the eggs inside. Point out the supplies, and say that you'd like the group to design and create a "nest" that will protect an egg—an unhatched bird—even if the nest falls from the top of a tall tree.

Tell group members these rules:

• They may design and create more than one nest, but for each nest they may use only fifteen straws, a handful (about a cup) of Easter grass, and two feet of duct tape.

• Every person in the group must be involved in both designing the nest and building the nest. It's up to the students to make sure that everyone has an opportunity to participate.

For a Greater Challenge

Have the students use rubber bands instead of duct tape in the construction of their nests. When using rubber bands, students will have to more carefully design and build their nests.

- The egg itself may not be wrapped with tape or Easter grass. In other words, the egg may be cushioned with the grass, but students may not wrap the grass and tape directly around the egg as padding.
- The students must place the egg inside the nest *after* they've built the nest.

When everyone understands the rules, allow the group to begin planning. Remind students of the rules if necessary—especially the rule that everyone in the group must participate.

When the group has finished planning, have all the students work together to build each nest. In other words, two students shouldn't work on one nest while three students work on another; they should all work on each nest.

There is not just one correct solution to this problem—any number of nest designs may work. One way to go about it is to construct a small, oval-shaped inner chamber with the drinking straws fairly close together; this inner chamber will hold the Easter grass and the egg. The inner chamber is surrounded by a square outer chamber that absorbs most of the shock when the nest hits the ground. Most likely, your teenagers will come up with creative ideas without any input other than initial encouragement.

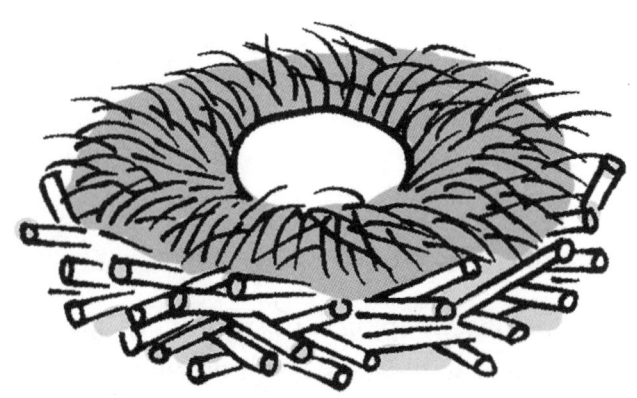

When group members have built the nests and put in the eggs, take everyone to the testing site. If students will be dropping the nests out of a window, have a couple of students drop the nests while the other group members gather outside a safe distance away from where the nests will fall. If students will be dropping the nests from a ladder, have only one student climb up the ladder, stopping at least two steps below the top. Have two people hold the ladder for support.

Then have group members drop the nests and let students survey the results. Encourage group members to discuss which design elements worked well and why. At least one of the students' initial designs will probably work well, but allow the group to build another nest if all the eggs broke.

Afterward, thank the group members for their efforts on behalf of the birds. Ask everyone to help clean up the area. Then gather group members together.

Ask:

- **In what *effective* ways did you work together to solve this problem?**
- **In what *ineffective* ways might people try to solve problems?**
- **How was each person important to the problem-solving process?**
- **Do you agree or disagree with the statement "Two heads are better than one"? Explain.**
- **Why are we sometimes hesitant to work together to solve problems?**

If teenagers had significant problems during the exercise—if they weren't able to build a nest that adequately protected an egg, for example—be sure to have the group discuss those aspects of the activity as well. For example, ask:

- **How should we determine whether an attempt to solve a problem was successful or unsuccessful? Why?**

After the discussion, distribute Bibles. Have students look up Romans 12:3-8, and ask a volunteer to read aloud the Scripture.

Then ask:

- **If people tried to solve problems using the guidelines in this Scripture, what would the problem-solving process look like?**
- **How effective do you think the process would be? Explain.**
- **What can be difficult about following these guidelines?**
- **What about these guidelines is important to remember as we work within our group? Why?**

- **How can we better look to one another when we have problems to solve?**

In closing, have group members thank one another for specific contributions people made during the problem-solving process.

[end] . . . . .

Scripture

"For by the grace given me I say to every one of you: Do not think of yourself more highly than you ought, but rather think of yourself with sober judgment, in accordance with the measure of faith God has given you. Just as each of us has one body with many members, and these members do not all have the same function, so in Christ we who are many form one body, and each member belongs to all the others" (Romans 12:3-5).

Servanthood Splash

Topic: Servanthood
Scripture: John 13:1-16
Supplies: Bibles; large, shallow tub filled with water; twelve doormats; towels

[start] . . . . .

As the group gathers, inform students that they will be trying to carry a large tub of water from one side of the room to another without spilling the water. They must, however, walk to the other side of the room by stepping only on the doormats. The group members will need to strategize and work together to decide where the mats will be placed, who will carry the tub, and how. (If you're in a small room, have students use fewer doormats.)

Once the group has accomplished the task, have students gather in a circle for discussion.

Ask:
• **What was most challenging about this activity? Why?**
• **How would this activity have been different if you had been asked to do it by yourself?**
• **How would you feel if you had been asked to do this for someone else?**

Ask students to open their Bibles to John 13:1-16. Invite several students to read the passage aloud as others follow along.

After students have read the Bible passage, say: **We may wonder why Jesus washed the disciples' feet. But in first-century Judea, there was no indoor plumbing, no running water in homes, and a person who entered a house, after removing his or her sandals, was given a basin of water to wash in. This lowly task was often performed by a house servant. Washing someone's feet was a most humble chore—it was a common, everyday, dirty task. When Jesus washed the disciples' feet, he was not only performing a chore, but he was demonstrating the heart of a servant.**

Ask:
• **What is surprising about Jesus washing the disciples' feet?**
• **In what ways does this chore seem far removed from our lives today?**

For a Greater Challenge

This activity may be made more challenging by setting a time limit on the activity or by making a rule as to how far apart the doormats must be placed.

- How did the disciples react to Jesus washing their feet?
- Why do you think they responded as they did?
- What did Jesus say to them?
- What is the most important thing Jesus wanted to teach his disciples through this act?
- Why do you think Jesus used this form of demonstration to show the nature of servanthood?
- Do you think Jesus particularly enjoyed this demonstration of servanthood? Why or why not?
- Do you think the disciples felt comfortable? Why or why not?

Ask group members to consider ways they might serve one another or other people in their community or school.

Then ask:

- As you think about having a servant's heart, what are some activities others might need your help with this month?
- Where do you see other opportunities to help people in the coming weeks?
- How would being a servant to others be a means of sharing the love of Jesus?
- How does serving someone else challenge you to go outside your "comfort zone"?
- Where do you see your own giftedness intersecting with the needs of others?
- How could you help to serve in your home, at school, or on the job?
- How can we serve each other in this group?

Challenge everyone in the group to silently make a commitment to serve at least one person in the coming week.

As a closure for this unity-building discussion, hold a foot-washing ceremony or some other demonstration of servanthood, such as washing one another's hands. Use the tub of water you used earlier, and have towels available. Invite the group to pray aloud for one another or for others in the community or church.

[end] . . . . .

Signed, Sealed, Delivered

Topic: Respect

Scripture: Matthew 7:12-14

Supplies: Bibles, wrapping paper, scissors, newsprint or chalkboard, marker or chalk

start] • • • • •

For this activity, you'll need a carpeted room large enough for students to safely form a human sculpture. Before students arrive, cut a sheet of wrapping paper into small squares. You'll need one square for each person.

Challenge teenagers to use their bodies to form a sculpture of a gift. Here are some ideas for ways group members might do this activity:

- shape themselves like a gift package

For a Greater Challenge

Give the group specific items and have students form human sculptures that show how to give themselves in ways that are symbolized by those items. Here are some examples:

• Give group members a ball and ask them to form a human sculpture that represents how to give the gift of fun.

• Give group members a teddy bear and ask them to form a human sculpture that represents how to show caring in a hard, cruel world.

• Give group members a book and ask them to form a sculpture that represents how they can give the gift of truth without looking like know-it-alls.

Allow students to be creative, and let them explain their sculptures when they've finished.

• shape themselves to show the feelings people have when they receive a gift

• shape themselves to depict actions they could perform as gifts to the group

The main requirement is that *everyone* must be part of the human sculpture.

Help the group members shape their human sculpture. Then ask the students to remain in their positions and describe what they shaped and why. Once they've finished their explanation, invite students to have a seat on the floor.

Have a volunteer read Matthew 7:12 aloud while the others follow along in their Bibles. Then have each person think of a physical item and tell how that item can represent that person giving himself or herself as a gift.

Say: **Think of yourself as a gift for a moment. In Matthew 7:12 we discovered God's directive to treat others as we want to be treated—how can you give yourself in that way? Think of a physical item that represents a way you want to give yourself.**

For example, teenagers might say,

• "I can make an effort to help others have fun, as represented by a ball."

• "I can invite people over and help them feel welcome in my home, as represented by a teddy bear."

• "I can listen to someone's story, as represented by a music box."

• "I can help friends with their homework, as represented by a book."

• "I can give biblical insights and true knowledge, as represented by a Bible."

Say: **We all want friends who give themselves to us and who welcome the gift of ourselves to them.**

Ask:

• **Why, when we all want this, do so few people give this?**

Ask each person to state a different reason why so few people give themselves to each other and welcome others as gifts. As teenagers share ideas, write the reasons on a chalkboard or a piece of newsprint displayed where everyone can see it.

Say: **In Matthew 7:12-14 we discovered that problems like the ones we've named have been going on for a long time. Not many people in Bible times obeyed God's directive to treat others as they would like to be treated, and not many people do so today. It's a narrow road that few people choose.**

Ask:

• **How can we overcome pressures that keep us from giving ourselves in caring ways and receiving others' care?**

Ask each person to share at least one idea, and encourage students to avoid repeating what others have said. Teenagers might come up with ideas like the following:

• Dare to be caring rather than assume it's "cheesy" to be nice.

• Recognize that a real man cares rather than giving in to the pressure to be macho.

• Remember how we want to be treated.

• Decide to deliberately obey God's directive to "do to others what you would have them do to you."

Then ask:

• **When have you felt like hiding your gifts or pretending they're not important?**

• **Why might people choose to give of themselves no matter what other people think or do?**

Give each person a small square of wrapping paper. Say: **You are a gift specifically given by God. Let this wrapping paper remind you to wrap yourselves well and deliver yourselves lovingly to people who will cherish the gifts you give. You are worth it, and choosing carefully who you give yourselves to will remind you of your worth.**

Stronger Than Thread

Topic: Friendship
Scripture: Proverbs 17:17
Supplies: Bibles, thread, rope, scissors, masking tape, markers

[start] •••••

Before students arrive, set up an obstacle course in your meeting area. If possible, set up the furniture in five rows, as in the following description:
- a row of furniture that students will climb over
- a row of furniture that students will have to run around once
- a table that students have to crawl under
- a table that students have to climb over
- a row of furniture that students have to crawl under

If you can't set up the furniture as described, create your own obstacle course that will be challenging for your group.

When students arrive, have them form pairs.

Say: **Friendship is one of the most powerful things you'll ever experience in your life. Today we're going to experiment with two different types of friendship. We'll reflect on what types of friendships we have and what types of friendships we should strive to have.**

Give each pair a piece of thread. Ask partners to stand side by side and tie their ankles together as they would in a three-legged race. When pairs are ready, have them gather at the beginning of the obstacle course.

Say: **Every friendship goes through tough times. Today your "friendship" with your partner is going to go through a very difficult time—let's see how well you stay tied together. There are no awards in this game for first place. Rather, we'll cheer for pairs who are able to stay tied together through the course.**

Give students a signal to begin. When participants arrive at the end of the course, cheer for pairs who were able to stay tied together.

Say: **That was one test of friendship. Let's try another.**

For a Greater Challenge

Instead of having students form pairs, have them form trios and tie themselves together to complete the obstacle course.

Give each pair a length of rope and ask partners to tie their ankles together as before. Then have pairs gather at the beginning of the obstacle course, and give them the signal to begin. When all the pairs have completed the course, have them gather in the center of the meeting room and sit in a circle.

Ask:
- **Which held up better—the thread or the rope? Why?**
- **If you could choose to be bound to your best friend with rope or thread, which would you choose? Why?**
- **What is the significance of the thread breaking easily?**

Read Proverbs 17:17.

Ask:
- **What does this verse say about friendship?**
- **Why is it important to include God in our friendships? Explain.**
- **Does this passage describe a friendship made with thread or rope? Explain.**
- **When have you experienced the type of friendship described in this passage?**
- **How can we exhibit this kind of friendship in our group?**

Have students sit in a circle on the floor and put the pieces of rope in the middle of the circle. As students are sitting, give each student a piece of masking tape and a marker. Ask each person to think of one element that makes a friendship strong and write it on the masking tape. When they've finished, have students tape their ideas to one of the pieces of rope. Then say: **I'd like you to take a moment to listen to the things that you all think are part of a great friendship.**

Give students time to read their ideas. When they've finished, say: **These are great ideas! Do you notice what's happening here? You've been bound together by ideas that make for great friendships. Today you've not only discovered what makes a strong friendship, you've discovered that great friendships exist in this room.**

Ask students to spend time praying for the friendships that they have with others the room. Then close the meeting with a short prayer. As students are leaving, encourage them to take home the pieces of rope with their ideas.

[end] . . . . .

Scripture

"A friend loves at all times, and a brother is born for adversity" (Proverbs 17:17).

Survival

Topic: Servanthood
Scripture: Acts 4:32-35
Supplies: Bibles, paper, pens or pencils, one photocopy of the "Survival" handout (p. 96)

[start] • • • • •

Give each person a sheet of paper and a pen or pencil. Ask participants to reinvent themselves as fictional characters. Students should not choose pre-existing people or characters; instead, they should make up the characters. Instruct each person to select a name, choose a vocation, and list any special talents or experience this character possesses. Explain that participants will be playing their characters in the following scenario.

Say: **Our group boarded a small plane for a tour of a distant land. The pilot was forced to make an emergency landing because a swarm of angry bees entered the cockpit. Fortunately, the pilot was able to land the plane on a remote island. But unfortunately, during the landing, the aircraft and the radio gear were damaged beyond repair.**

Then say: **Use the next ten minutes to detail a strategy for survival and rescue. Work together to discuss how you will meet the basic needs of food, clothing, and shelter. Your plan should include the contributions of all of the fictional characters in the group and how the characters' skills and experience equip them for their responsibilities.**

Give students a copy of the "Survival" handout (p. 96). Take a moment to discuss the specifications of the surroundings given on the handout. You may choose to prompt teenagers with the following questions.

Ask:
• **What will you eat? How will food be obtained and prepared?**
• **How will you stay warm and dry?**
• **How will you be protected from dangerous animals, snakes, and insects?**

For a Greater Challenge

To help participants appreciate the importance of serving one another, encourage individuals to take the island activity a step further. When the group has finished its survival and rescue strategy, ask each participant to come up with a plan detailing how he or she would survive alone on the island.

- **How will you obtain and store water?**
- **How will you be rescued?**

When teenagers have finished, have them share their plan for survival.

Then ask:

- **Would the average person find it harder or easier to survive if he or she was stranded on the island alone?**
- **What were the benefits of having several people working together to survive?**
- **What were some specific ways that people served others in the group?**
- **Why was serving others practical and necessary?**
- **How would you respond to someone who wasn't doing his or her part to help the group?**
- **How would you respond to someone who expected to be served rather than to help?**

Read Acts 4:32-35 aloud.

Ask:

- **In what ways did your island simulation resemble the behavior of people in the early church?**
- **How did the church model Christ's example of servanthood?**
- **How was the world impacted by early Christians' devotion to one another?**
- **What are some ways the church serves its members today?**
- **What are some ways the church serves the community and the world?**
- **What are some things you see individuals doing today to serve the body of Christ?**

Say: **This passage points out that because of the early Christians' devotion to one another, no one was needy.**

Ask:
- Could that statement be made of our church—that we're so devoted to one another that no one is in need? Explain.
- Why were service and sharing necessary for the survival of the early church?
- What makes service an essential part of our faith and witness today?
- What are some needs of others that we can meet as a group? as individuals?
- How can serving the needs of others be a blessing to you?

Say: **By serving one another, we can meet needs that might otherwise distract from the work of the church. Not only will the church benefit, you will receive many blessings as well—returned favors and the fulfillment that comes from doing right.**

end] . . . . .

Scripture

"All the believers were one in heart and mind. No one claimed that any of his possessions was his own, but they shared everything they had" (Acts 4:32).

Survival

Temperature: 40 to 70 f

Current Climate: rainy season

Animals: fish, bears, rabbits, squirrels, bats, snakes

Other Available Food: mushrooms, olives, berries, honey

Supplies available on the plane: one first-aid kit, three parachutes, four blankets, one box of twenty-five matches, three life preservers, one pocket knife, one ten-foot rope

Taste Test

Topic: Respect
Scripture: Exodus 20:13-17
Supplies: Bibles, slips of paper, pen or pencil, tape, chairs, three different brands of cola (such as the two major national brands and a store brand), three small cups for each person, permanent markers, chenille wires

[start] • • • •

Before this activity, write these Bible verses on slips of paper, one verse per slip: Exodus 20:13; Exodus 20:14; Exodus 20:15; Exodus 20:16; and Exodus 20:17. If you have more than five students, duplicate verses as necessary so that each student will have a slip of paper. Then tape one slip of paper underneath each chair.

Pour three different brands of cola drinks for each person. Mark the cups "1," "2," and "3" and make sure that all the cups labeled with the same number contain the same type of cola.

Set out permanent markers, and give each person the three different types of cola. Tell teenagers which three brands of cola you've given them without specifying which brand is in which cup.

For a Greater Challenge

Don't tell participants which three cola brands you're using. Instead let students guess which brands you used as they try to identify which is which.

Say: **Work together to figure out which brand of cola is in which cup. Write on each cup the brand of cola you think is in that cup. As a group, talk over your techniques for doing this.** Teenagers might compare sugar content, use their past experience to identify a personal favorite, take a poll, or use another strategy.

Allow several minutes for teenagers to work together on this project. When students have finished, ask them to report their conclusions and the methods they used to form those conclusions. Then tell kids how accurate their results were.

Ask:

• **Which strategies do you think were most accurate? Why?**

Say: **Each strategy had its strengths and weakness, and together we could have used any of those strategies to guess which cola was in which cup. But the thing that really determined what was in each cup was the true identity of the cola. In a similar way, we can use hints to tell us whether people truly have respect for others around them—but only that person and God will know the real motive behind the person's actions and attitudes.**

Under your chairs are five actions that demonstrate respect for others. These verses from the Bible are the last five of the Ten Commandments. These five commandments should govern how we treat other people.

Tell students to look under their chairs, and have them remove the slips of paper. Then let students read aloud the Bible verses. If you have fewer than five people, read the remaining references yourself, or give them to people who want more than one verse to work with.

Give each person a chenille wire and say: **A ring is a symbol of commitment, and commitment is shown through action. Use this chenille wire to make a ring with a symbol that shows how to demonstrate respect in the manner referred to in your Scripture verse. Try phrasing the verse as a positive action rather than as something we should not do. For example, for Exodus 20:13 you might say, "Value each life" instead of "Do not murder," or for Exodus 20:14 you might say "Honor family relationships" instead of "Do not commit adultery."

Give teenagers a few minutes to work on their rings. Then ask everyone to show the rings and tell what the symbols mean.

Then ask:

• **What difference would it make in the world if more people demonstrated the type of respect your verse outlines?**

• **How could you express respect in our group according to the verse you read?**

• **Which verse do you think people disobey most often? What would convince you to obey that commandment?**

• **When has someone shown respect for you in a way that has made a difference in your life?**

• **What are some ways you can make a difference by showing respect to others?**

• **How will you be sincere in the way you treat others?**

Scripture

"You shall not murder. You shall not commit adultery. You shall not steal. You shall not give false testimony against your neighbor. You shall not covet your neighbor's house" (Exodus 20:13-17a).

Tinfoil Teamwork

Topic: Unselfishness
Scripture: James 4:1-3
Supplies: Bibles, paper sack, several rolls of aluminum foil, paper, pens or pencils

[start] . . . . .

Have everyone sit in a circle, and set a paper sack in the center of the circle. Give students each a small piece of foil. Ask students to tear up the foil into tiny pieces and put the pieces into the paper sack.

Then say: **I'm going to give you more foil, and I want you to make it so you can't tear it into pieces. In fact, I want you to make it so strong that you can lift one of the members of our group with it.**

Give teenagers the roll of foil. Challenge students to work together to make a device they can use to lift one member of the group. One way to do this is to twist the foil into ropes and have students hold the ends of the foil ropes while another student sits on them. The more foil ropes the group members create and the tighter they twist the ropes, the stronger the seat becomes. Students might even want to weave the foil ropes together. Your group may come up with even better ideas.

Allow teenagers to work on the project for several minutes, then have them demonstrate the lifting process. Congratulate the students on their efforts.

Say: **When we live only for ourselves, our lives are weak like the foil—we fail to connect with other people and we fail to make a difference in the world. But when we live unselfishly, we connect with other people, and we all become stronger.**

Ask:

- **What do you think made this project work** (or not work)?
- **What is it like to lift people up emotionally in real life?**
- **What makes living for others better than living for ourselves?**

Have each person share at least one reason that unselfishness is better than selfishness.

For a Greater Challenge

Challenge teenagers to see how little foil they can use to lift a group member. Give students only a small amount of foil, then add more as they need it to make their foil chair strong enough to lift a person.

Make sure each student has a Bible, and say: **Search James 4:1-3 for examples of both selfish and unselfish approaches to life.**
Ask:
- **What are some ideas in these verses that show a selfish approach to life?** (Some examples include "you want something but don't get it," "you cannot have what you want," and "you ask with wrong motives.")

Ask:
- **What is the one phrase that describes an unselfish approach to life?** ("Ask God.")

Ask:
- **How could each of the selfish approaches be changed to unselfish approaches, ones that promote togetherness and godliness?** (Some examples include "think about what others want rather than just what I want," "ask with right motives," and "put my pleasures in perspective and work for the good of the whole group.")

Ask:
- **Why is selfishness wrong?**
- **What damage does selfishness do to a group?**
- **How does selfishness damage the person who acts selfishly?**

Say: **The only time we don't mind selfishness is when we're the ones being selfish.**
Ask:
- **Why is it harder to notice our own selfishness than the selfishness of others?**

Give each person a piece of paper and a pen or pencil, and ask teenagers to spread out as far as the room allows. Have students write a confession to God about an area in their lives in which they have been selfish. These confessions might range from taking the biggest brownie to using someone sexually. Then carefully gather up the papers so no one can read what another student wrote. Let students talk to you about these if they want to, but think beforehand what you'll do if a student brings up a sensitive issue.

Say: **I've gathered up your selfishness. From here on we can deliberately show unselfishness. I'll give you a piece of foil, and I'd like you to shape it to show a deliberate action you can take to show unselfishness in this group. The one requirement is that the foil must stay in one piece.**

If youth have trouble with this activity, help them by asking questions such as "What does unselfishness look like?" "What does it act like?" and "How do you know it when you see it?" Point out that the reason for the activity is to show that unselfishness can be seen.

When students have finished their foil sculptures, encourage people to display what they've made. As each person shows his or her foil creation, affirm a specific way it shows unselfishness. Point out that even affirming another person's creation is a way to show unselfishness.

Have youth combine their foil creations into one large symbol of unselfishness in the group. Instruct them to connect the pieces together without tearing the foil.

Hold up the foil chair youth created with their unselfish actions at the beginning of this session. As you poke the foil full of holes with a pen or pencil, say: **Selfishness pokes holes in the good we create through unselfishness.**

Ask:

• **How will you refuse to "poke holes" in the good around you?**

• **How will you keep from letting holes be poked in your own actions?**

Say: **Sometimes it's possible to keep others from being selfish, and doing so is one of the most powerful ways to show love.**

Ask:

• **What are some ways to keep others from being selfish?**

Say: **It's important to realize, though, that we can't always stop someone else from being selfish. Ultimately each of us chooses to be selfish or unselfish.**

Reread James 4:1-3 aloud.

Ask:

• **Why would you not want to be the kind of selfish person described in this passage?**

• **How will you keep from being selfish when you're in this group? at home? at school?**

Give each person a piece of foil to take home, and say: **Cherish the people around you as if they're as fragile as this foil.**

Tiny Power

Topic: Encouragement

Scripture: Hebrews 10:24-25

Supplies: Bibles, lots of toothpicks (the flimsier, the better), two hymnbooks or other heavy books, chalkboard or newsprint, chalk or marker

[start] • • • • •

Hold up a box of toothpicks and a hymnbook or another heavy book. Ask students how many toothpicks they think it will take to support the hymnbook. Tell the group members the challenge will be to stand the toothpicks up and lay the hymnbook on top of the toothpicks. Have teenagers see how few toothpicks they can use to get the hymnbook to stay up without wobbling or falling. Encourage everyone to help in deciding the placement of the toothpicks and how many to use. Once they've put their toothpicks in place, participants will probably have to hold the toothpicks to support the hymnbook.

When group members finish setting up the toothpicks and hymnbook, bump the book so it falls or push it so the toothpicks break. Say: **I want the hymnbook to be supported even when it gets bumped or has extra pressure on top. This time, support the hymnbook so I can put another hymnbook on top and it will still stand.** Pass out new toothpicks if needed, and urge everyone to work together to decide the placement and the number of toothpicks to use.

For a Greater Challenge

Have teenagers search the room for items that would give more support to the hymnbooks. Then have them tell how this extra support is like encouragement. They also might tape some toothpicks horizontally on a slippery floor to provide stops for the upright toothpicks—this might be like using two different kinds of encouragement, words and smiles, to support others. Or students might tape two toothpicks together so the toothpicks will be less flimsy—this is like two people working together to encourage others.

Ask:
- **How many more toothpicks were needed this second time?**
- **What, besides bumping the book or adding extra weight, might make this project require more toothpicks?**

Say: **Now use your entire supply of toothpicks to support the hymnbook. Feel free to let toothpicks support toothpicks or do whatever you need to make the foundation strong.**

When students have finished, admire their work and have them tell you about the strategy they used.

Say: **You have just demonstrated the idea of encouragement. Encouragement is something you can never have enough of. It's something we can be creative in giving so that others always have a storeroom of encouragement to draw on. Listen to Hebrews 10:24-25 for ideas you demonstrated in your toothpick activity.**

Read Hebrews 10:24-25 aloud. Then ask students to choose encouraging phrases from the verses and explain how they demonstrated those phrases in the activity.

Students might give some of the following answers:
- "Let us consider"—Group members devised strategies to set up the toothpicks.
- "We may spur one another on"—They prompted one another to set up the toothpicks a certain way.
- "Let us not give up"—Students had to keep trying to support the book. They may have broken some toothpicks in the process, but they replaced those with new ones.
- "All the more as you see the Day approaching"—When students knew there was another book to be placed on top, they used more toothpicks. The "Day" in this passage is seen by some as the Day of Judgment, and things may get harder before that day.

Congratulate group members on their insights, then say: **These toothpicks represented words of encouragement and actions of encouragement. We all need encouragement to show love and do the good deeds we're designed to do. The greater the pressures, the more we need encouragement.**

Ask:

• **What are your favorite *actions* of encouragement to give? to receive?**

• **What are your favorite *words* of encouragement to give? to receive?**

Say: **Encouragement is something we have to keep on giving—people need encouragement every day.**

Ask:

• **Why do you think people need ongoing encouragement?**

• **How can you make certain you keep giving encouragement?**

As students respond to these questions, emphasize the importance of sticking with others and continuing to care for them through good times and bad times.

Say: **Sometimes church is the place where people find the least encouragement. So let's be encouraging on purpose.**

Ask:

• **What three steps—or rules—could we come up with for encouraging others in our group?**

Suggest to the students that they refer to Hebrews 10:24-25 as they come up with steps or rules to follow in the group. Write students' ideas on a chalkboard or a piece of newsprint so that everyone can see them. Teenagers might suggest ideas such as "encourage everybody, not just the people you know best"; "remember the power of your words"; or "say things you'd want to hear."

Give group members each a toothpick to carry with them, and gather teenagers in a group hug while you pray: **God, thank you for the power of encouragement. Help us to use it in ways that help people feel as close to others as we all are standing close right now.**

To the Top

Topic: Encouragement

Scripture: Romans 15:1-7

Supplies: Bibles, a two-by-four for each pair (boards should be about three feet long), markers

[start] • • • • •

Explain to students that they're each going to get a turn climbing as high as they want to, using only the two-by-fours and their fellow students. Ask the group how they think they might accomplish this task and what things might be important as they work on this task.

Then have students form pairs. Have the partners face each other, and have pairs line up shoulder to shoulder to form two lines of students, as in the illustration. Then give each pair a two-by-four, and ask one student to hold each end. Have partners stand so that they are holding the boards horizontally.

For a Greater Challenge

Add an element of trust to this activity by having the climber wear a blindfold. If you do this, be sure to place a thick safety mat underneath the entire area. You may even want to have the volunteer wear a helmet.

Explain that one volunteer will climb up the boards as the other students hold the boards. The first pair will hold its board close to the floor so that the climber can step up on it. The next pair can hold its board a little higher, and so on. Explain that the students and the boards will easily bear the climber's weight. Ask a volunteer to begin as the first climber (you may need to take his or her place holding a board). As the climber clears a "rung," have the pair holding that rung move to the other end of the line and hold their board up to continue making the "ladder."

Allow the volunteer to climb as high as he or she would like (or as high as group members' arms will reach). Then help him or her down, and ask other students to try the activity. Continue until everyone who would like to try has had a chance to climb. Be very sensitive to students who don't want to do this activity. Some young people will believe they're too heavy for the others to support them. As students climb, notice what group members say to each other and to the climbers.

When everyone has finished, ask:

- **What was it like to climb the ladder?**
- **What was it like to hold the rungs for others as they climbed during this activity?**
- **What role did encouragement play as you did this activity? If group members didn't encourage you, what difference might it have made if they had?**
- **Volunteers, would you have been willing to attempt this climb if the other group members had not been encouraging? Explain.**
- **How could the rungs of the ladder be like encouragement for others?**
- **Why is it important to encourage each other?**
- **How could encouragement among group members make our group stronger?**

Give everyone a Bible, and have the group work together to find and read Romans 15:1-7.

Ask:
- What does this passage tell you about encouraging one another?
- According to this passage, what are some specific ways we can encourage others in this group?
- The last verse in this passage talks about the foundation of encouragement, which is accepting each other. Why is this sometimes so difficult?
- How can we as a group be more accepting and encouraging toward one another?

Say: **It often seems easier to put others down than to build them up. We had a chance in our activity to build each other up. Now I'd like to issue a challenge to you for the coming week. If you feel the urge to put someone down or say something unkind about someone, stop yourself, think about this activity and the Scripture we read, and try to build that person up instead. Next time we meet, I'd like to hear about what happened.**

Give each person a marker, and have students write prayers on the boards, asking God to help them be encouraging to other people during the coming week.

[end] . . . . . .

Scripture

"We who are strong ought to bear with the failings of the weak and not to please ourselves. Each of us should please his neighbor for his good, to build him up" (Romans 15:1-2).

Tread on Me

Topic: Servanthood
Scripture: Philippians 2:3-8
Supplies: Bibles

start] •••••

Clear an area of the room. Then have group members line up shoulder to shoulder, all facing the same direction. Have students spread out so that, with their arms outstretched, they can just touch the hands of the people on either side. Students should stand with their feet about shoulder-width apart.

Designate a home area about three feet past the last person at one end of the line. Explain to the group that its goal is to get every member to the home area. Then tell the group the following rules:

• Other than where their feet are currently touching, no one may touch the floor anywhere else in the room.

• No one may jump or otherwise use solely his or her own power to reach the home area.

• No one may "sacrifice" himself or herself for the group. In other words, one person cannot volunteer to carry everyone else to the home area and then be disqualified because his or her feet touched the ground. All the group members must be in the home area in order to be successful.

For a Greater Challenge

Have the group perform the activity on a low, long balance beam. (Playgrounds at many parks have such balance beams.) Add a rule that no one may touch the ground. This activity will require additional planning and caution by group members. While teenagers are planning, encourage them to anticipate problems and devise solutions to those problems ahead of time. For example, have students think of what they will do someone loses his or her balance.

Encourage students to plan what they'll do before moving. As group members are discussing strategy, you can refine the rules. For example, you can let teenagers know that they don't have to remain on their feet or in the exact positions they're currently in; they can't touch the floor elsewhere in the room, but they can sit or lie on the floor where they're at. Or you can let teenagers know that they may take off their shoes if a strategy they come up with would be too difficult to carry out with shoes on.

One way to accomplish this task is to have the person farthest from the home area step on the feet of the person next to him or her. Both people grasp hands and lean away from each other so their weight is evenly distributed. The moving person steps in the same way to the next person, and so on down the line. Then the person who is now farthest from home repeats the process. This continues until everyone reaches the home area.

After the students have chosen a strategy, have them begin. Supervise the teenagers as they carry out their plan, being ready to support group members if needed. For example, if the strategy requires group members to step on each other's feet, you could stand ready to help if someone starts to fall.

When everyone has reached home, have group members applaud for themselves and give each other high fives. Then gather everyone together.

Ask:

- **How did you serve each other during this activity?**
- **What's difficult about being a servant to others?**
- **What positive things happen to a person who serves?**
- **What positive things happen to a person who is served by others?**

Ask a volunteer to serve the rest of the group by reading aloud Philippians 2:3-8 while the other students follow along.

Then ask:
- **What does this passage teach about servanthood?**
- **How can we serve one another?**
- **Outside of our meetings, how have others in our group served you? What was that like?**
- **What positive things can happen to our group if we focus on serving one another?**

Have the group members stand up and form a circle. Close the activity by having each person bow slightly and tell what he or she can do to serve the group. If a group member has trouble thinking of a way he or she can serve, encourage others to suggest ways that the person has served others in the past.

Scripture

"Your attitude should be the same as that of Christ Jesus: Who, being in very nature God, did not consider equality with God something to be grasped, but made himself nothing, taking the very nature of a servant, being made in human likeness. And being found in appearance as a man, he humbled himself and became obedient to death—even death on a cross!" (Philippians 2:5-8).

Unscrambled Scriptures

Topic: Respect
Scripture: 1 Peter 2:17
Supplies: Bibles, index cards, marker, basket or small box, T-shirts, permanent markers or fabric paint

[start] •••••

Before this activity, choose several Bible verses. Each verse should have a word count of at least double the number of teenagers you expect. (For example, if you expect five teenagers, use verses with at least ten words.)

Next clearly write the first several words of one Bible verse on an index card, the next several words on a second card, and so on for the remainder of the verse. When you've finished with that verse, you should have a card for each student. Write several more verses on index cards, and keep the cards for each verse in separate piles.

For Matthew 28:19, you might use five cards: on one card write, "Therefore go and make disciples"; on the second card, "of all nations"; on the third card, "baptizing them in the name"; on the fourth card, "of the Father and of the Son"; on the last card, "and of the Holy Spirit."

Put all the cards for one verse in a basket or a small box. Have each participant draw one card. Instruct students to arrange themselves in the correct order of the words in the verse. Once everyone is in order, have each participant read aloud his or her part of the verse.

Repeat the activity a few more times with different verses.

Then ask:

• **What made this activity successful?**

• **How would you describe the way you treated each other as you worked to accomplish your goal?**

• **What would have happened if people had refused to demonstrate respect for each other during this activity?**

Say: **In life, as in this activity, it's important to respect everyone. It's hard for people to accomplish their goals without respecting one another. That also goes for how we treat each other in this group. If we're going to be a strong group, we've got to respect one another.**

For a Greater Challenge

Try giving students index cards from several verses, and have them put the cards in order while sorting out which cards belong in which verses.

Read 1 Peter 2:17.
Ask:
- **Why do you think it's important to respect everyone?**
- **How does respect help others know what we believe?**
- **What types of people are hard for you to respect? Explain.**

(Caution students against naming names or otherwise identifying specific people—instead have students talk in general terms.)

- **When have you felt like you weren't respected? What did that feel like?**
- **How can we show respect to people in this group?**
- **How can we show respect to people outside this group?**

Say: **For Christians, respect should be something like a piece of clothing we wear all the time. Let's create "respect shirts" as a way of displaying our commitment to be respectful at all times as a reflection of Christ.**

Give each person a T-shirt, and set out permanent markers or fabric paints. Instruct students to decorate their T-shirts with words and pictures to illustrate the concept of respect. Encourage teenagers to especially focus on ways they can show respect to people who are hard for them to respect.

When students have finished decorating their T-shirts, let them gather around the shirts and spend time praying aloud for the strength to respect others in the ways they've shown on their T-shirts. Encourage group members to take their shirts home to remind them of the commitments they've made.

Water Works

Topic: Unselfishness
Scripture: John 6:1-14
Supplies: Bibles, bucket of water, glasses of various sizes (one for each participant), liquid measuring cup

[start] • • • • •

In this challenge, students will be trying to fill various-sized glasses with equal amounts of water. Before this activity, you'll need to fill a bucket with water. One way to do this so that the activity will work is to first fill the smallest glass with water. Then multiply the amount in that glass by the total number of glasses (participants) you will have. For example, if the smallest glass holds ½ cup of water and you have ten glasses, you'll need to pour five cups of water into the bucket.

Give each person a glass and say: **Divide up the water in the bucket so that each participant has exactly the same amount. You must use all of the water in the bucket.**

When the group has finished dividing up the water, use a measuring cup to measure the amount of water in each glass. Have teenagers each take note of how much water is in their glass, then let students continue working to fill all the glasses equally. Measure the amount of water in the glasses as many times as participants ask you to.

When students have finished dividing the water equally, say: **In life, we don't all have the same advantages and challenges. Each of us is created differently and faces a different set of circumstances. But we all have something to offer other people. When we share the unique blessings God has given us instead of living only for ourselves, we help make life better for others. Just as in this activity, if we refuse to share with others, everyone loses.**

Ask:

• **What are some different situations people might be born into?**
• **Who are some people who have overcome adversity to accomplish something great?**
• **How is God able to use someone from any situation to accomplish his will?**

Then read John 6:1-14 aloud and say: **Jesus distributed bread and fish among the people the way you divided the water. But**

For a Greater Challenge

To make this activity more challenging, fill the bucket with syrup instead of water.

there was an endless supply. One boy's contribution of two fish and five loaves fed five thousand men and probably at least that many women and children.

Ask:
- How would this account have been different if the boy had decided to keep his food?
- Why did God make more than enough food?

Say: **God took what the boy offered and blessed thousands of people through the boy's act of generosity.**

Ask:
- How can you demonstrate that kind of unselfishness in your life?
- What sorts of things do people often hope to achieve in their lifetimes?
- What kind of selfish goals do we often set?
- How can a life offered to God bless many people?

Say: **If God can make so much out of a couple of fish and a few loaves of bread, there is no limit to what he can accomplish through the life of a person dedicated to his service. Many people live for success and many accomplish their goals. But these achievements are small compared to all God could do through their lives if they lived unselfishly.**

Ask:
- Why do we sometimes doubt the ways God can use our lives for service?

Say: **When the boy offered his food to Jesus, he still got to eat. And he enjoyed added blessings—he became a hero who is remembered in Scripture to this day. He felt the gratitude of those he helped feed, the privilege of being used by God, and the excitement of watching a real miracle.**

Ask:
- How will your life be changed if you offer your time, talents, and resources to the Lord?

Allow time for students to share any commitments they have made about living their lives for God instead of solely for themselves. Close in prayer, asking God to multiply this gift and bless others through these contributions.

What's Mine is Yours

Topic: Unselfishness
Scripture: Romans 12:9-18
Supplies: Bibles, large shopping bag

[start] • • • • •

As students arrive, ask each person to discreetly place a personal item (such as a bracelet, a ring, a set of keys, a charm, a CD, or a shoe) into a shopping bag. Group members should not be able to see what other students place in the bag.

Begin the challenge activity by gathering the teenagers into a large circle. Place the bag in the center of the circle, and ask the group to work together to try to return each item to its rightful owner. Tell teenagers that they cannot reveal which item is theirs until the end of the game.

Set a time limit for the game—up to ten minutes—and see how many of the items students can correctly pair with their owners. Then let each student reveal which item he or she originally placed in the bag. Once everyone has his or her original object, ask these questions:

- **What made this challenge difficult?**
- **How many of you saw objects you would have liked to own yourself?**
- **How many of you grew anxious wondering if your item would be returned to you?**
- **In what ways do you think people in our culture have difficulty sharing?**
- **In what ways might ownership be a major obstacle to sharing and helping each other?**
- **What unique challenges do you see to being a Christian for a person who has great wealth?**

Following the discussion, distribute Bibles and invite someone to read aloud Romans 12:9-18.

Then ask:

- **How does this Scripture passage illustrate the need for us to be unselfish?**
- **What is involved in being unselfish?**

For a Greater Challenge

To really get your group working together, don't allow students to talk during the challenge activity. Let teenagers use hand movements or nonverbal communication only. You might also consider placing a ten-dollar bill in the sack.

- **What are some practical ways this Scripture talks about sharing and being unselfish?**
- **How can these points help us live as unselfish people?**
- **Which of these aspects of sharing are easiest to fulfill? Which are most difficult?**
- **What key words in this passage might help you remember the nature of sharing?**
- **Other than material possessions, what else are we encouraged to share with others?**
- **What are some positive things we receive when we learn to give?**
- **What are some challenges to sharing you believe we face in this group? What can we do to overcome these challenges?**

Using the key words from the Scripture passage, ask the students to list ways the group could share with others. Suggestions might include collecting canned goods for a local food pantry (Romans 12:13), forming a prayer chain (Romans 12:14), or thinking of ways to involve people who may feel left out or unimportant (Romans 12:16). If possible, set up a date or time for the group to complete some of these sharing activities.

Close the time together with prayers for people throughout the world who work to meet the needs of others (Romans 12:10-11).

When Talk Turns Tacky

Topic: Love

Scripture: James 2:14-19

Supplies: Bibles, at least two balloons per person, slips of paper, pens or pencils, masking tape, straight pin, permanent markers

[start] . . . . .

Give each person a balloon, a slip of paper, and a pen or pencil. Explain to students that they will work together to write loving sentences on the slips of paper, put a different slip of paper in each balloon, blow up the balloons, and then try to keep all the balloons in the air at the same time.

For a Greater Challenge

Have students pretend they're human "words" that stick. Find a Velcro wall in a church, museum, or fun center. Have youth put on the equipment that lets them stick to the wall.

After everyone has had a chance to stick to the wall, ask:
- **What makes it possible for us to stick to the wall?**
- **What would make us fall off the wall?**
- **What Velcro words—words that stick people together—can we use more often in our group?**
- **What actions would give those words sticking power?**
- **How is failing to show love like trying to stick to the wall without Velcro?**

Give each person a strip of Velcro (available at craft and fabric stores) to take home to remind teenagers to stick words to caring actions.

Say: **Choose things you would say to a friend, not to a date or in a boyfriend/girlfriend relationship. After you write a loving sentence on a slip of paper, roll up the paper and put it in a balloon.** Challenge teenagers to put the papers inside the balloons so the papers can be read through the sides of the balloons. Students might try shaking the balloons to get the papers to unroll.

As group members work to keep all the balloons in the air at once, they'll discover that they must work together to do this. After students have kept the balloons in the air for a couple of minutes, congratulate everyone. Say: **When we work together, we can say loving words to each other and really mean what we say. We can create an atmosphere that avoids making loving words seem cheesy or sappy.**

Ask:

- **What do you like about sincerely spoken words that are loving?**

As each person gives a different reason, use masking tape to stick his or her balloon to the wall. Continue until everyone has responded and all of the balloons are taped to the wall.

Say: **Sometimes loving words lose the ability to stick. This happens when people don't match loving actions to loving words.**

Ask:

- **What do you dislike about people who talk lovingly but don't act that way?**

Each time someone gives a reason, use a straight pin to pop one of the balloons.

Say: **Loving words that aren't accompanied by loving actions are no more than hot air. They burst and hurt people similar to the way these popping balloons hurt our ears. Let's see what James 2:14-19 has to say about this.**

Read James 2:14-19 aloud as students follow along.

Ask:

• **What does this Scripture passage say about loving words that aren't accompanied by loving actions?**

As teenagers respond, help students rephrase statements to match Scripture. For example, teenagers might say, "words without works do no good," "words without caring actions are dead," "we do no good if we don't follow up words with actions," "even the devil can say holy words, and we know where he really stands!" or "I show real love and faith through good deeds."

Say: **Failing to act nice is one of the main problems in youth groups. It's also a severe way to disobey God. Refusing to act nice destroys unity faster than almost anything else. It's like trying to fill up a cup that has no bottom. Most Christians who fail to act lovingly don't do it on purpose—they're not mean people. They just ignore certain people, for example, like when they talk to their friends and forget to talk to others. Let's name ways to be deliberately nice so we don't accidentally act mean.**

Give each person a new balloon. Have students take turns naming deliberate actions they will take to build unity in the group. Each time a group member names a caring action that no one else has said, he or she can blow one puff of air into the balloon. Challenge each person to be the first to fill his or her balloon with caring actions.

When everyone has filled a balloon and tied it off, ask:

• **Can competing to be nice to people ever backfire? Explain.**

• **What would be advantages of working to outdo one another in doing good?**

Give students permanent markers, and have teenagers remember the actions they came up with as they filled their balloons. Challenge them each to use the first letter of several of the caring actions to spell a word, then have them write the word on their balloons.

This example spells SAY:

• **S**eat a new student between you and a good friend. Then when you talk, the new person is right in the middle of the action.

• **A**lways speak to everyone who attends. Deliberately acknowledge every person, recognizing that both new and longtime members need to feel loved in our group.

• <u>Y</u>ell, "Hi, [first name]!" to everyone who enters the room. When people arrive, we want them to hear their names.

Ask:
- **Why are loving actions important to our group?**
- **How will you be deliberate in your loving actions?**
- **What part of James 2:14-19 do you most want to memorize?**

Pray for each person by name, asking God to help that person refuse "tacky" talk and replace it with talk that builds unity. Your prayer might go like this: "God, please help Pattie, Jeff, Paula, Larnelle, Lucy, and me use our words to unite rather than to be tacky. Help us change tacky talk into unifying talk. Thanks. Amen."

Scripture

"What good is it, my brothers, if a man claims to have faith but has no deeds? Can such faith save him?...Faith by itself, if it is not accompanied by action, is dead" (James 2:14, 17b).

Works of Art

Topic: Cooperation

Scripture: 1 Corinthians 12:4-11

Supplies: Bibles, photocopies of a simple drawing, folding chairs with hard seats, boxes of crayons, watch with a second hand

[start] • • • • •

Before this activity, create a simple drawing like those in coloring books. Photocopy the picture, making enough copies for everyone in the group. Then arrange chairs in a circle in your meeting area—one chair for each group member. Place a photocopy of the picture and a box of crayons on each chair. Choose a signal you'll use to get players' attention during the activity, such as clapping your hands, blowing a whistle, or turning the lights off and on.

Tell students that the challenge of this activity is for everyone to become an artist! Each person will contribute his or her artistic abilities and help color the pictures on the chairs. First demonstrate your signal to the group so players will easily recognize it during the challenge—remember, their attention will be focused elsewhere.

Explain how the challenge works. When you give the signal, each person will kneel in front of a chair in the circle and begin to color part of the picture. When you give the signal again, players will move to the right and begin coloring the picture they find on that chair. Give the signal about every fifteen seconds until all the pictures have been completed. Encourage players to color as neatly as they can. The goal is to make the pictures as nice as possible.

When the pictures are finished, have players pick up the pictures and sit on the chairs. Go around the circle and let each person display the completed picture from his or her chair. You might consider having group members vote on which picture is the best.

Ask:

• **How does each picture represent the work of the whole group?**

• **How did cooperating on the pictures make the artwork more interesting?**

For a Greater Challenge

To make this activity more challenging, give the signal and have students move to the next station more frequently than every fifteen seconds.

* **What would have happened if you had each worked on your own picture, but one of you couldn't color very well?**
* **How did cooperating during this challenge activity bring us together as a group?**
* **How would our goals change if we committed to cooperating with one another more often?**

Give everyone a Bible. Have group members look up and read 1 Corinthians 12:4-11.

Then ask:

* **What does this passage say about cooperation?**
* **Why do you think God gave us different gifts?**
* **How does it make you feel to know that although we all have different gifts, the same Spirit gave those gifts to us?**
* **What do you think your gift is?**
* **How can you use that gift for God? How can this group help you?**
* **How can cooperating with one another help further the kingdom of God? How would it change our lives?**

Have group members place their pictures on their chairs again. Then have everyone go around the circle and sign each picture so that each picture will have the signature of every group member who contributed to the artwork. Encourage group members each to take home the picture they started. The pictures will remind students to cooperate with one another.

Indexes

Scripture Index

OLD TESTAMENT

Exodus 20:13-17	97
Exodus 35:4–36:7	46
Leviticus 19:18	7
1 Kings 21:1-20	21
2 Chronicles 19:7	77
Proverbs 17:17	90
Proverbs 18:24	19
Ecclesiastes 4:9-12	63
Jeremiah 33:3	52

NEW TESTAMENT

Matthew 7:12-14	87
Mark 10:35-44	24
John 6:1-14	114
John 13:1-16	85
John 15:12-17	66
Acts 4:32-35	93
Romans 2:11	77
Romans 5:6-11	71
Romans 12:3-8	81
Romans 12:9-18	116
Romans 15:1-7	106
1 Corinthians 1:20-25	33
1 Corinthians 12:4-11	122
1 Corinthians 13:4-7	66
2 Corinthians 6:3-10	74
Ephesians 2:19-22	16
Ephesians 4:2-6	49
Ephesians 4:14-16	13
Philippians 2:1-4	30
Philippians 2:3-8	109
Colossians 3:12-14	10
1 Thessalonians 5:9-11	44
2 Thessalonians 2:16-17	39
Hebrews 3:12-14	58
Hebrews 10:24-25	103
James 1:5	33
James 1:5-8	68
James 2:14-19	118
James 4:1-3	100
1 Peter 2:17	112
1 Peter 4:8-11	61
1 John 3:16-17	42
1 John 3:18	55
1 John 4:7-21	27

Topical Index

Cooperation
Connected Acrobatics 30
Fort Fun 46
Geometric Designs 49
Jumping Jack Flash 61
Lean on Me 63
Works of Art 122

Encouragement
Eternal Encouragement 39
Foot-to-Foot Pass 44
Hold On 58
Tiny Power 103
To the Top 106

Friendship
Bound in Unity 10
Bridges of Friendship 16
Building Bonanza 19
Reconciling Ties 71
Stronger Than Thread 90

Love
Acts of Love .7
Common Bond Clues 27
Group Hug 55
Loving Touch 66
When Talk Turns Tacky 118

Problem Solving
Boxed In 13
Crossword Conundrum 33
Great Unknown 52
Puzzling Problems 68
Safety Nests 81

Respect
Circle of Friends 24
R-E-S-P-E-C-T 77
Signed, Sealed, Delivered 87
Taste Test .97
Unscrambled Scriptures 112

Servanthood
Removing Obstacles 74
Servanthood Splash 85
Survival 93
Tread on Me 109

Unselfishness
Candy Craze 21
Everybody Up 42
Tinfoil Teamwork 100
Water Works 114
What's Mine Is Yours 116

Exciting Resources for Your Youth Ministry

At Risk: Bringing Hope to Hurting Teenagers
Dr. Scott Larson

Discover how to meet the needs of hurting teenagers with these practical suggestions, honest answers, and tools to help you evaluate your existing programs. Plus, you'll get real-life insights about what it takes to include kids others have left behind. If you believe the Gospel is for everyone, this book is for you! Includes a special introduction by Duffy Robbins and a foreword by Dean Borgman.

ISBN 0-7644-2091-7

All-Star Games From All-Star Youth Leaders

The ultimate game book—from the biggest names in youth ministry! All-time no-fail favorites from Wayne Rice, Les Christie, Rich Mullins, Tiger McLuen, Darrell Pearson, Dave Stone, Bart Campolo, Steve Fitzhugh, and 21 others! You get all the games you'll need for any situation. Plus, you get practical advice about how to design your own games and tricks for turning a *good* game into a *great* game!

ISBN 0-7644-2020-8

The Youth Worker's Encyclopedia of Bible-Teaching Ideas

Here are the most comprehensive idea books available for youth workers. With more than 365 creative ideas in each of these 400-page encyclopedias, there's at least one idea for every book of the Bible. You'll find ideas for retreats and overnighters...learning games...adventures...projects...affirmations... parties... prayers... music...devotions...skits...and more!

                    Old Testament   ISBN 1-55945-184-X
                    New Testament   ISBN 1-55945-183-1

Awesome Worship Services for Youth

These 12 complete worship services involve kids in 4 key elements of worship: celebration, reflection, symbolic action, and declaration of God's Truth. Flexible and dynamic services each last about an hour and will bring your group closer to God.

ISBN 0-7644-2057-7

Discover our full line of children's, youth, and adult ministry resourses at your local Christian bookstore, or write: Group Publishing, P.O. Box 485, Loveland, CO 80539. www.grouppublishing.com

More Resources for Your Youth Ministry

New Directions for Youth Ministry
Wayne Rice, Chap Clark and others

Discover ministry strategies and models that are working in *real* churches...with *real* kids. Readers get practical help evaluating what will work in their ministries and a candid look at the pros and cons of implementing each strategy.

ISBN 0-7644-2103-4

Hilarious Skits for Youth Ministry
Chris Chapman

Easy-to-act and fun-to-watch, these 8 youth group skits are guaranteed to get your kids laughing—and listening. These skits help your kids discover spiritual truths! They last from 5 to 15 minutes, so there's a skit to fit into any program!

ISBN 0-7644-2033-X

Character Counts!: 40 Youth Ministry Devotions From Extraordinary Christians
Karl Leuthauser

Inspire your kids, introduce them to authentic heroes, and help them celebrate their heritage of faith with these 40 youth ministry devotions from the lives of extraordinary Christians. These brief, interactive devotions provide powerful testimonies from faithful Christians like Corrie ten Boom, Mother Teresa, Dietrich Bonhoeffer, and Harriet Tubman. Men and women who lived their faith without compromise, demonstrated Christlike character, and whose true stories inspire teenagers to do the same!

ISBN 0-7644-2075-5

On-the-Edge Games for Youth Ministry
Karl Rohnke

Author Karl Rohnke is a recognized, established game guru, and he's packed this book with quality, cooperative, communication-building, brain-stretching, crowdbreaking, flexible, can't-wait-to-try-them games youth leaders love. Readers can tie in these games to Bible-learning opportunities or just play them.

ISBN 0-7644-2058-5

Discover our full line of children's, youth, and adult ministry resources at your local Christian bookstore, or write: Group Publishing, P.O. Box 485, Loveland, CO 80539. www.grouppublishing.com

Essential Lessons for Youth Ministry!

The 13 Most Important Bible Lessons for Teenagers

Ground your kids in the basics of the Christian faith! You'll use active learning to answer questions such as "Who is God?," "Who is Jesus?," and "What is the church?" PLUS: Step-by-step meeting plans, photocopiable handouts, and discussion questions are included!

ISBN 1-55945-261-7

Living Beyond Belief: 13 Bible Studies to Help Teenagers Experience God

These solid, in-depth Bible studies for youth ministry display how God's presence affected the lives of biblical people. As teenagers explore Sarah, Jacob, Ruth, Martha, Zacchaeus, and others, they'll see how God affects their everyday lives as well. Each 45- to 60-minute lesson includes active and interactive learning experiences, as well as worship time.

ISBN 0-7644-2099-2

Understanding God Together: 13 Bible Studies for Youth Ministry

Specially designed for small groups and small churches! These 13 dynamic meetings explore essential attributes of God and help kids see how those attributes touch their lives. Includes tips for adapting ideas to younger and older teenagers, and easy-to-use, photocopiable handouts.

ISBN 0-7644-2101-8

Faith on Fire: 15 Lessons to Help Teenagers Change the World

Debbie Gowensmith and Helen Turnbull

These innovative lessons show teenagers how to make a difference by caring for God's creation through community service and through global outreach. Plus, they'll see how the Bible applies to their everyday lives, in their community, and around the world. With practical help, fun activities, and action ideas, teenagers will be changing their world in no time!

ISBN 0-7644-2077-1

Discover our full line of children's, youth, and adult ministry resources at your local Christian bookstore, or write: Group Publishing, P.O. Box 485, Loveland, CO 80539. www.grouppublishing.com